40 Days to Discovering God's Big Idea for Your Life

BOOKS BY MYLES MUNROE

Applying the Kingdom

God's Big Idea

In Pursuit of Purpose

Kingdom Parenting

Kingdom Principles

Maximizing Your Potential

Myles Munroe 365-Day Devotional

The Glory of Living

The Purpose and Power of Love & Marriage

The Purpose and Power of Praise & Worship

Rediscovering the Kingdom

Releasing Your Potential

Single, Married, Separated and Life After Divorce

Understanding Your Potential

Waiting and Dating

AVAILABLE FROM DESTINY IMAGE PUBLISHERS

40 Days to Discovering God's Big Idea for Your Life

A Personal Devotional Designed to Change Your Life

Myles Munroe

Compiled by Angela Rickabaugh Shears.

Destiny Image® Publishers, Inc.
P.O. Box 310
Shippensburg, PA 17257-0310

"Speaking to the Purposes of God for this Generation and for the Generations to Come."

Bahamas Faith Ministry
P.O. Box N9583
Nassau, Bahamas

For Worldwide Distribution, Printed in the U.S.A.

ISBN 10: 0-7684-2730-4
ISBN 13: 978-0-7684-2730-1

This book and all other Destiny Image, Revival Press, MercyPlace, Fresh Bread, Destiny Image Fiction, and Treasure House books are available at Christian bookstores and distributors worldwide.

For a U.S. bookstore nearest you, call **1-800-722-6774.**
For more information on foreign distributors, call **717-532-3040.**
Reach us on the Internet: **www.destinyimage.com.**

1 2 3 4 5 6 7 8 9 10 / 12 11 10 09 08

Contents

Introduction 7

Day 1   God's Kingdom on Earth 9

Day 2   God's Original Intent 13

Day 3   Your Home Base 17

Day 4   His Kingdom Come 21

Day 5   Why Not Earlier—Or Later? 25

Day 6   Do as the Romans Do 29

Day 7   Good Seed and Bad Seed 33

Day 8   The Power of the Garden Principle 37

Day 9   He Is in Control 41

Day 10 Earth's Only Legitimate Culture. 45

Day 11 Culture Power 49

Day 12 Declaration of Independence 53

Day 13 The Master Gardener 57

Day 14 Carrying Out the King's Will 61

Day 15 Our Governor, the Holy Spirit 67

Day 16 Fulfilling His Promise. 73

Day 17 Who Is Tending Your Garden? 77

Day 18 Seeking and Saving the Lost. 83

Day 19 Self-government Disasters 87

Day 20 Illegal Resident 93

Day 21   Kingdom Influence. 97

Day 22   Expanding Your Influence Through Prayer 103

Day 23   Praying for Yeast 109

Day 24   Priceless Treasure. 115

Day 25   Pride and Independence 119

Day 26   "Bring Them Here to Me" 123

Day 27   Culture Revelations (Part 1) 127

Day 28   Culture Revelations (Part 2) 131

Day 29   Dreaming. 135

Day 30   Reflected Glory. 141

Day 31   Community = Common Unity. 145

Day 32   A Lesson to Learn. 149

Day 33   The Principle of Engagement 153

Day 34   Heaven Is Not Our Priority (Part 1). 159

Day 35   Heaven Is Not Our Priority (Part 2). 163

Day 36   Engaging the World. 167

Day 37   Living in Two Worlds. 171

Day 38   Transformation 175

Day 39   A Just and Righteous King. 181

Day 40   Victory Through Service. 187

Introduction

This devotional journal is a continuation of the concepts and principles presented in *God's Big Idea*. God's idea originated in the mind and heart of the Creator and was the motivation and purpose for the creation of the physical universe and the human species. His idea is superior to all the collective wisdom and ideas of human intellect. It is an idea that is beyond the philosophical reserves of human history and supersedes the institutions that govern humankind since his first human society.

This 40-day devotional journal is designed to help you discover how *God's Big Idea* includes you. God wants to make the Earth a place of Kingdom harmony and peace and He would like you to be a part of His plan.

Each day is divided into four inspiring and thought-provoking sections:

- Scripture—relevant and life-changing words from God.
- Devotion—excerpts from *God's Big Idea*.
- Considerations—questions and ideas for thoughtful pause.
- Meditation—thoughts that prompt introspection and action.

Each day brings you closer to discovering God's love and plan for you, including how to fulfill your destiny now; enjoy continuous fellowship with the Lord; turn the Earth into a place filled with His culture; and how you can make a positive difference in what happens on Earth.

You will experience for yourself through personal devotion and journaling how to be directly involved in *God's Big Idea* by helping to plant and multiply His garden communities where all God's children live fruitful and abundant lives.

God's Kingdom on Earth

GOD BLESSED THEM AND SAID TO THEM, "BE FRUITFUL AND INCREASE IN NUMBER; FILL THE EARTH AND SUBDUE IT. RULE OVER THE FISH OF THE SEA AND THE BIRDS OF THE AIR AND OVER EVERY LIVING CREATURE THAT MOVES ON THE GROUND" (GENESIS 1:28).

TODAY'S DEVOTION

R eligion is man's idea, not God's.

God's original idea is much bigger and much better than anything we humans could ever dream up. And what was God's big idea? He decided to extend His heavenly Kingdom to the earthly plane, to expand His supernatural realm into the natural realm. Or, to put it another way, God decided to fill the Earth with the culture of Heaven.

How did God bring His big idea into being? In this, as in almost everything else He does, God did the unexpected. Typically, human kingdoms and empires rise—and fall—through war and conquest. Not God's. Because His thoughts are not our thoughts and His ways are not our ways (see Isa. 55:8), God did something completely different. When God decided to bring the culture of Heaven to Earth He did not use war. He did not use conquest. He did not issue a code of laws. No, when God set out to bring Heaven to Earth, He did something much simpler, something uniquely beautiful and wonderful.

He planted a garden.

(*God's Big Idea*, Chapter One)

CONSIDERATIONS

1. Can you think of three earthly kingdoms that have risen and fallen? Name them and the reason for their ultimate demise.

2. In what ways has religion failed humankind?

3. What is the "alternate government" that will change the world?

4. Because many cultural conflicts are religiously based, what can be done to help solve the differences in ideologies?

5. How can you personally tap into God's big idea to help change your world for the better?

MEDITATION

*God initiated His Kingdom on earth by planting
a Garden in Eden, a place specially prepared as the
habitation for the first human representatives of His
Kingdom government on earth. From this hub of abundance
and beauty, they would follow their government's mandate
to "**Be fruitful and multiply**" (Gen. 1:28 NKJV), filling
the Earth with their kind and planting Kingdom "gardens"
wherever they went. In this manner, like leaven in bread, they
would infuse the territory of Earth with the nation of Heaven.*

(*God's Big Idea*, Chapter One)

Are you willing to plant a garden in your neighborhood or your city?

What could your first step be?

God's Original Intent

THE HEAVENS DECLARE THE GLORY OF GOD; THE SKIES PROCLAIM THE WORK OF HIS HANDS (PSALM 19:1).

TODAY'S DEVOTION

*I*ntent can be defined as "original purpose." It is more important for us to know what a person intended, than to know what he or she said. If we do not properly discern intent, misunderstanding will follow. This is one reason why there are so many confused people in the world. Because we have misunderstood God's original intent, we have misunderstood not only ourselves, but also God's purpose for us on earth.

Intent is also the most critical component of motivation. It is the source of motivation and the reason why someone does something or creates something. Unless specifically stated, however, intent is usually hidden. A good example of this is a work of art by a master painter. Artists rarely state their intent plainly; they let their art speak for itself. For those who take the time and effort to search it out, the intent behind an artist's work can be discerned from the painting itself. No other explanation is necessary.

(*God's Big Idea*, Chapter One)

CONSIDERATIONS

1. Do you agree that "if intent is unknown, misunderstanding is inevitable"? Have your intentions been misunderstood by others? What was the result?

2. God's intentions are found in the Bible. Cite several Scripture passages that clearly reveal God's intent for your life.

3. Most religions focus on trying to get God's attention, which is the wrong approach. In what ways have you tried to get God's *attention*, instead of trying to discover His *intention*?

4. Have you had a special revelation from God that has brought you deeper understanding of His intent for your life or that of a loved one? Explain.

5. God speaks to you through His creation and His Word—list several ways in which you open your heart and mind to what He has to say to you.

MEDITATION

The phrase "God said," [see Genesis 1:26-28], indicates that what follows is the expression of the intent that God purposed beforehand in His mind. Whenever God speaks we need to listen carefully, because we are about to receive His hidden intention. In this case, we learn God's intention—His purpose—in creating the universe, the planet we call Earth, along with all its creatures, and especially, the human race.

(*God's Big Idea*, Chapter One)

Many times God's intentions are misunderstood—how does that affect our purpose and response to His voice?

Your Home Base

Now the Lord God had planted a garden in the east, in Eden; and there He put the man He had formed. ... The Lord God took the man and put him in the Garden of Eden to work it and take care of it (Genesis 2:8,15).

TODAY'S DEVOTION

G od's original intent was to colonize Earth with Heaven.

I understand that most people today think of colonization in very negative terms, particularly those who have lived under colonial rule, as I have. And with good reason: throughout history almost all human colonization has been characterized by coercion, brutality, greed, exploitation, victimization, and oppression. These traits, in fact, reflect the nature and tactics of satan, the original enemy of humanity, who illegally seized control of God's original garden "colony," and deposed its rightful rulers, Adam and Eve.

Colonization was God's original idea, but His colony on earth took the form of a garden. As an analogy, a garden shares the same general traits as a colony, but without all the negative baggage. In sharp contrast to the violent and forceful way human empires expand, God's way was much more subtle. Just as a garden gradually, beautifully, and completely transforms the fallow ground where it is planted, the influence of God's Kingdom on Earth grows gradually and often invisibly until eventually it will fill the earth, infusing it with the culture of Heaven.

(God's Big Idea, Chapter One)

CONSIDERATIONS

1. Jesus likened the process of Kingdom growth to the way yeast leavens bread (see Matt. 13:33). Are you experiencing a continual, gradual spiritual growth?

2. How does establishing Kingdom gardens fulfill His ultimate goal to fill the Earth with His glory?

3. When God created humankind He gave us rulership over the Earth, but He never gave us ownership. What is the difference between the two?

4. Is it possible for God's full glory to be manifested on the Earth? Why or why not?

5. Because Jesus' mission was to reestablish the Kingdom of Heaven on Earth, His first recorded public words were, "Repent, for the kingdom of heaven is near" (Matt. 4:17b). How do you think this message applies to His mission?

MEDITATION

*As the initial outpost of God's invisible Kingdom
in the visible realm, Eden was a touch of Heaven
on Earth. Everything about it reflected Heaven's
culture, government, and ways. Truly, it was paradise.
Unfortunately, this idyllic state of affairs did not last long.*

(*God's Big Idea*, Chapter One)

Establishing His glory within your personal garden is what He desires.

Is your home base in God's Kingdom on Earth?

His Kingdom Come

Our Father in heaven, hallowed be Your name, Your kingdom come, Your will be done on earth as it is in heaven (Matthew 6:9-10).

TODAY'S DEVOTION

God's big idea was to reproduce the Kingdom of Heaven in the visible realm by planting a Kingdom outpost on the Earth and populating it with Kingdom citizens who would govern according to Kingdom government, live according to Kingdom culture, and expand Kingdom influence until it filled and transformed the Earth. Politically speaking, the term for this kind of governmental expansion is *colonization*. As a Kingdom outpost on Earth, Eden was a *colony* of Heaven established by a righteous, just, and benevolent King who is compassionate, gracious, slow to anger, and abounding in love (see Ps. 103:8).

(*God's Big Idea*, Chapter One)

DAY 4—*His Kingdom Come*

1. List the four similarities between Heaven and Eden before the Fall.

2. Why did God create the Earth before creating Adam?

3. Why is it essential for a nation to share a common language?

4. Without laws, a constitution, and moral convictions what does a nation consist of?

5. Common values bind a nation together—why?

MEDITATION

That is still God's big idea—and His purpose
for today. God is still in the horticultural business.
All Kingdom citizens share a common call and
commission from their King to be royal gardeners,
sowing seeds and planting "gardens" of Kingdom
culture and government throughout the world until "the
earth shall be filled with the knowledge of the glory of
the Lord, as the waters cover the sea" (Hab. 2:14 KJV).

(*God's Big Idea,* Chapter One)

Are you willing to become a royal gardener, or are you too comfortable with the way things are? What would change your mind?

Why Not Earlier—Or Later?

BUT DO NOT FORGET THIS ONE THING, DEAR FRIENDS: WITH THE LORD A DAY IS LIKE A THOUSAND YEARS, AND A THOUSAND YEARS ARE LIKE A DAY. THE LORD IS NOT SLOW IN KEEPING HIS PROMISE, AS SOME UNDERSTAND SLOWNESS (2 PETER 3:8-9).

TODAY'S DEVOTION

Between the time that Adam and Eve lost the earthly outpost of the Kingdom of Heaven to satan the pretender and the time Jesus Christ appeared announcing its restoration, thousands of years passed. Why did God wait so long before reestablishing His Kingdom on Earth? Why did He allow so much time to pass? Why was Christ born in the particular time in history in which He appeared? Why not earlier—or later?

In answering these questions we must understand first of all that God views time and history differently than we humans do because He is bound by neither. From the perspective of eternity, God can take all the "time" He needs to accomplish His purposes.

(*God's Big Idea*, Chapter Two)

DAY 5—*Why Not Earlier—Or Later?*

1. Has the timing of circumstances and situations ever caused you to wonder if God's hand was holding the clock still?

2. List a few times when you thought something like, *Wow—that was perfect timing!*

3. How was Rome a model for God's plan for Kingdom expansion?

4. In what ways did Jesus legitimize Roman authority?

5. In what ways do you legitimize your national government's authority?

MEDITATION

God waited to send His Son to the Earth until an earthly kingdom appeared that looked, however imperfectly, like His own, so that when Jesus preached about the Kingdom, everyone would know what He was talking about. Christ came at the right time, into the right setting, into the right culture, into the right kingdom, and into the right environment because He was preaching exactly what was happening in the world under the Roman Empire.

(*God's Big Idea*, Chapter Two)

Are you sometimes frustrated with your earthly government?

What lessons can be learned from Jesus' example?

Do as the Romans Do

"Show Me the coin used for paying the tax." They brought Him a denarius, and He asked them, "Whose portrait is this? And whose inscription?"

"Caesar's," they replied.

Then He said to them, "Give to Caesar what is Caesar's, and to God what is God's."

When they heard this, they were amazed. So they left Him and went away (Matthew 22:19-22).

TODAY'S DEVOTION

A nother way Jesus acknowledged the legitimacy of the Roman form of government is the fact that He used a portion of that form as a model for establishing His own government on earth—His church.

Whenever the Romans set up their government in a new territory, they sent a *procurator,* or governor, to rule the province in the name and authority of the emperor. At the time of Jesus' public ministry, Pontius Pilate was the procurator of Judea. In addition, the Romans borrowed many ideas of government from the Greeks, modified them, and made them their own. One of these was the idea of a "called-out" assembly of citizens who met democratically over matters of common concern. Both the word and the concept would have been familiar to the people of Jesus' day; the concept because they saw it in action regularly in everyday government, and the word because of its frequent appearance in the *Septuagint,* the Greek translation of the Old Testament that was in common use in Jesus' day, where it referred specifically to the children of God.

(*God's Big Idea,* Chapter Two)

CONSIDERATIONS

1. In what way is the Church, Christ's Body on Earth, a governmental body rather than a religious body?

2. Is Jesus a religious leader or a government agent on a Kingdom mission? How does this concept change your perspective about Him?

3. Contrary to popular belief, the "Great Commission" is not a religious statement but a declaration of government policy. As a Kingdom government appointee, how will you carry out this responsibility?

4. The church Jesus established is not a religious institution but a governmental agency charged with publicizing and implementing Kingdom principles and policies throughout the Earth. In your opinion, how have His appointees succeeded...or failed?

5. List a few ways in which the deceiver distorts the Kingdom government's role and responsibilities.

MEDITATION

...All authority in heaven and on earth has been given to Me. Therefore go and make disciples of all nations, baptizing them in the name of the Father and of the Son and of the Holy Spirit, and teaching them to obey everything I have commanded you. And surely I will be with you always, to the very end of the age (Matthew 28:18-20).

(*God's Big Idea*, Chapter Two)

How does this Scripture passage speak to your heart...to your mind...to your spirit?

Good Seed and Bad Seed

THE ONE WHO SOWED THE GOOD SEED IS THE SON OF MAN. THE FIELD IS THE WORLD, AND THE GOOD SEED STANDS FOR THE SONS OF THE KINGDOM. THE WEEDS ARE THE SONS OF THE EVIL ONE, AND THE ENEMY WHO SOWS THEM IS THE DEVIL. THE HARVEST IS THE END OF THE AGE, AND THE HARVESTERS ARE ANGELS (MATTHEW 13:37-40).

TODAY'S DEVOTION

There are two kinds of people in the world: those who are children of the Kingdom of Heaven, and those who are not. Christ Himself made this distinction clear in a teaching story He told about a farmer who planted good seed in his field. At night an enemy came and planted weeds in the midst of the wheat. No one was the wiser until the wheat and the weeds sprouted up together. The farmer told his workers not to pull up the weeds for danger of uprooting the wheat as well. Instead, he allowed both to grow until harvest time, when the weeds were gathered and burned, while the wheat was stored in the granary (see Matthew 13:24-30).

(God's Big Idea, Chapter Two)

DAY 7—*Good Seed and Bad Seed*

CONSIDERATIONS

1. Contrast the aspects of God's Kingdom of Heaven and the pretender's false kingdom. (Example: joy vs. fear)

2. Why is it that most religions, including Christianity, focus on preparing people to leave Earth rather than planting roots and "sticking around for a while"?

3. Do you believe you have been given the ability to make a positive difference in your realm of influence?

4. Are the weeds in your garden choking out the beauty of the seeds sown by the Master Gardener? Will you be willing to burn the weeds at harvest time?

5. When others look at the fruit of your life, can they see good-seed evidence? List a few of the seeds that you've been blessed to produce.

MEDITATION

As with many of His other stories, Jesus used here [Matt. 13:37-43a] a garden-like analogy to talk about the Kingdom of Heaven. And while the overall meaning of the story relates to the end of this present age, one thing that stands out clearly is the existence in the world of two distinct cultures: Kingdom culture and the culture of the "evil one," the pretender. Just as wheat and weeds are easy to tell apart, so too is Kingdom culture distinct from worldly culture.

Our lives should leave absolutely no doubt as to which culture we live under.

(*God's Big Idea*, Chapter Two)

Are you a royal Kingdom citizen or a slave in the evil one's culture?

DAY 8

The Power of the Garden Principle

AND A HIGHWAY WILL BE THERE; IT WILL BE CALLED THE WAY OF HOLINESS. THE UNCLEAN WILL NOT JOURNEY ON IT; IT WILL BE FOR THOSE WHO WALK IN THAT WAY; WICKED FOOLS WILL NOT GO ABOUT ON IT. NO LION WILL BE THERE, NOR WILL ANY FEROCIOUS BEAST GET UP ON IT; THEY WILL NOT BE FOUND THERE. BUT ONLY THE REDEEMED WILL WALK THERE, AND THE RANSOMED OF THE LORD WILL RETURN. THEY WILL ENTER ZION WITH SINGING; EVERLASTING JOY WILL CROWN THEIR HEADS. GLADNESS AND JOY WILL OVERTAKE THEM, AND SORROW AND SIGHING WILL FLEE AWAY (ISAIAH 35:1-10).

TODAY'S DEVOTION

Everyone in the world is looking for the Kingdom of Heaven, even though most of them don't realize it. People are not looking for religion. Buddhism does not satisfy. Hinduism does not satisfy. Islam does not satisfy. Judaism does not satisfy. "Religious" Christianity does not satisfy. Money and material riches do not satisfy. We were created to rule a garden domain, and we will never be content outside that environment. The King's garden expansion program is designed to draw many people into His Kingdom from all over the world and prepare them for Kingdom life and leadership in the "new heaven and...new earth" (Rev. 21:1) that He is already preparing.

(God's Big Idea, Chapter Two)

DAY 8—*The Powe of the Garden Principle*

CONSIDERATIONS

1. Life under the pretender's evil rule is characterized by greed, selfishness, hatred, violence, war, murder, envy, strife, lust, immorality, cruelty, brutality, empty religion, and oppression. List the characteristics of life in God's Kingdom:

2. Jesus preached a simple, pure message. Modeled after His, write your own mission statement.

3. The power to walk in authority comes from God. What steps can you take to avail yourself to His power?

4. Jesus imparted His power and authority to His disciples and they healed and spread the Gospel. In what other ways were the disciples empowered?

5. The power of the Garden Principle is irresistible because it is the power of the King, the Master Gardener. That same power lies within the hearts and lives of every Kingdom citizen—is it powerful enough to spread the Gospel worldwide?

MEDITATION

Jesus Christ came to Earth to reclaim the desert and transform it once more into a great garden, the vibrant life and abundance of which reflect the character, nature, and environment of His Father's heavenly Kingdom. He was an oasis—a garden in the desert—and He planted seeds of life, righteousness, and holiness that sprouted into other oases.

(*God's Big Idea*, Chapter Two)

Are you an oasis in the middle of the world in which you live?

He Is in Control

FOR THE FOUNDATIONS OF THE EARTH ARE THE LORD'S; UPON THEM HE HAS SET THE WORLD (1 SAMUEL 2:8).

TODAY'S DEVOTION

One time not long after national elections in the Bahamas, someone asked me in an airport, "What do you think about your new government?"

I replied, "I only have one government."

It doesn't matter who occupies the prime minister's chair or the Speaker of Parliament's chair or the governor's mansion; it doesn't matter who sits on the throne and is called king or queen. There is only one government, and it belongs to Him whose throne will never move or be toppled: Almighty God, the King of kings and Lord of lords. His rule in Heaven is eternal, without beginning or end. But He also created the Earth and established His Kingdom there as well.

(*God's Big Idea*, Chapter Three)

CONSIDERATIONS

1. The words *earth* and *world* are often used interchangeably, but they refer to two different things in First Samuel 2:8b, "For the foundations of the earth are the Lord's; upon them He has set the world." Describe the difference.

2. God rules directly in Heaven, but His plan for the Earth was to rule it indirectly through human representatives created in His own image. What were Adam and Eve's responsibilities?

3. In Romans 13:1-5, Paul makes it clear that God is the true authority behind human affairs. Can you name a few modern-day countries in which the government leaders defy the rule of God?

4. It is easy to think that satan is in control of some governments, but Scripture tells us differently. List 4-5 verses that declare the sovereignty of God in world affairs.

5. Write Isaiah 45:22-23 in your own words and explain what it means to you.

MEDITATION

*Satan the pretender may believe that he runs the show
and controls the governments of the Earth, but it is the
King of Heaven who guides human history and destiny toward
His desired ends. He raises up one power and brings down
another, all in accordance with His sovereign will and purpose.*

(*God's Big Idea*, Chapter Three)

Earth's Only Legitimate Culture

AS THE KING WAS WALKING ON THE ROOF OF THE ROYAL PALACE OF BABYLON, HE SAID, "IS NOT THIS THE GREAT BABYLON I HAVE BUILT AS THE ROYAL RESIDENCE, BY MY MIGHTY POWER AND FOR THE GLORY OF MY MAJESTY?"

THE WORDS WERE STILL ON HIS LIPS WHEN A VOICE CAME FROM HEAVEN, "THIS IS WHAT IS DECREED FOR YOU, KING NEBUCHADNEZZAR: YOUR ROYAL AUTHORITY HAS BEEN TAKEN FROM YOU. YOU WILL BE DRIVEN AWAY FROM PEOPLE AND WILL LIVE WITH THE WILD ANIMALS; YOU WILL EAT GRASS LIKE CATTLE. SEVEN TIMES WILL PASS BY FOR YOU UNTIL YOU ACKNOWLEDGE THAT THE MOST HIGH IS SOVEREIGN OVER THE KINGDOMS OF MEN AND GIVES THEM TO ANYONE HE WISHES." IMMEDIATELY WHAT HAD BEEN SAID ABOUT NEBUCHADNEZZAR WAS FULFILLED… (DANIEL 4:29-33).

TODAY'S DEVOTION

Human empires rise and fall, but the Kingdom of God stands forever. Earthly rulers who forget or who refuse to acknowledge the One to whom they are accountable set themselves up for judgment, and even destruction. Nebuchadnezzar, king of Babylon, ruled the mightiest empire the world had ever known up to that time, but even he had to learn to humble himself before the God of Heaven.

(*God's Big Idea*, Chapter Three)

CONSIDERATIONS

1. What caused the ultimate downfall of Nebuchadnezzar? Are there government leaders today who are guilty of this same attitude?

2. Many earthly governments are in disorder. This can be attributed to the following principle:

3. Human-based culture is illegitimate and rooted in evil and destruction. What can be done to recognize the legitimate Kingdom of God?

4. The clash between the illegitimate and legitimate cultures is continually felt worldwide, especially recently with the rise of terrorism, which is based, many times, on religious convictions. Are there ways you can make changes within your realm of influence?

5. Name other culture clashes we are faced with today, and describe how worldly governments have contributed to the legitimization of perversion.

MEDITATION

*The shrinking of our global community through
telecommunications technology and the Internet has
greatly accelerated the rate and intensity of culture clash.
A "take-no-prisoners" war is being waged for the soul
of our culture, and it is vitally important that we identify
the nature of the fight. What do we do when…we discover
that mosques are popping up next to churches all over America?
… The need to preserve democratic freedom and individual
rights conflicts with the need for greater security.*

*What do we do when the counterculture of sexual
perversion labors and lobbies vigorously to dignify
and legitimize itself through legislation? How should
we respond to the claim that two men or two women
should be able to marry each other, and to raise children
in such a same-gender household? … This is no time to
play religious games; the very life of our culture is at stake.…*

*We need help from beyond ourselves—help from the
Creator of the Earth's original and only legitimate culture.*

(*God's Big Idea*, Chapter Three)

How has the culture clashes affected your life, your
worldview?

Culture Power

Do not conform any longer to the pattern of this world, but be transformed by the renewing of your mind. Then you will be able to test and approve what God's will is—His good, pleasing, and perfect will (Romans 12:2).

TODAY'S DEVOTION

Culture is stronger than politics. It really doesn't matter who is in power. Politicians come and go, and governments rise and fall, but culture still remains. Culture is also more powerful than religion. One of the biggest challenges that Church leaders faced during the first few centuries of the Church's existence was how to keep those who were coming into the Church out of pagan backgrounds from bringing elements of their pagan culture with them and blending these with their new faith in Christ. Even today we continue to see the enormous power of culture in the fact that many believers and Kingdom citizens display lifestyles that differ little from those of people who make no claim to be in the Kingdom.

The United States of America has a rich historical heritage of faith and even today has the highest percentage of citizens who claim to be believers (Christians) of any of the industrialized nations. Yet every year in America, 500,000 unborn babies are aborted—*legally.*

(God's Big Idea, Chapter Three)

CONSIDERATIONS

1. The enormous power of culture affects the fact that many believers and Kingdom citizens display lifestyles that differ little from those of people who make no claim to be in the Kingdom. Why?

2. The power of culture trumps religion in its ability to shape the thoughts, values, and beliefs of people, and to influence their behavior and what they are willing to accept. How can impotent religion be replaced with empowering Kingdom authority?

3. How and why has homosexuality become a cultural norm in a country that professes to have more believers than any other industrialized nation?

4. Why did God think it was necessary to change the minds of the Israelites through presenting them with a set of Commandments?

5. How can reading—or not reading—the Bible change the culture of a nation?

MEDITATION

Culture is the manifestation of the collective thinking of a people. This means that whoever controls the minds of the people creates and controls the culture. Culture is also a product of law. The most effective way to change a culture is to control its laws, because whatever is instated into law eventually will become accepted as "normal" by most citizens, regardless of how they might have felt at the beginning. This is all part of the process of mind control.

(*God's Big Idea*, Chapter Three)

Are there laws you don't agree with? Is there a way to change them? Have you ever thought of getting involved in the political process as a way to control culture?

Declaration of Independence

THE GOD WHO MADE THE WORLD AND EVERY-
THING IN IT IS THE LORD OF HEAVEN AND
EARTH AND DOES NOT LIVE IN TEMPLES BUILT BY
HANDS (ACTS 17:24).

TODAY'S DEVOTION

Culture rests on the foundation of law. God's laws are not to restrict us, but to protect us and to ensure that His culture fills the Earth. This is what Adam and Eve forgot when they chose to rebel against the King in Eden. When they ate of the one tree in the Garden that God had placed off limits, they did more than commit personal sins for the sake of pleasure and enlightenment; theirs was an act of treason against the government of their Creator. Their disobedience was in fact a declaration of independence from God and His righteous, loving, and benevolent rule. Adam and Eve turned their backs on God's Kingdom in favor of setting up a regime of their own making. Unfortunately, satan the pretender illegally seized the throne, began pulling the strings, and imposed his own culture of hatred, murder, and deceit.

(*God's Big Idea*, Chapter Three)

CONSIDERATIONS

1. God issued laws for us to obey in His Kingdom which produce a community lifestyle that creates a totally unique society. How does accepting His laws enhance your life?

2. Why is it that some cultures can coexist and others can only clash?

3. It was never God's desire or intent that there be a British culture, or an American culture, or a Bahamian culture. He wanted a Kingdom culture, one culture throughout the entire created realm. Do you believe this will happen in your lifetime? Why or why not?

4. When Adam and Eve declared their independence from God's law, what was the ultimate result and who benefited?

5. List three things that the evil pretender steals from those who are under his rule.

MEDITATION

The Kingdom of Heaven is not about escaping Earth; it is about occupying the planet. As Kingdom citizens, we are destined to change this world. In the name of Jesus the King, nations and peoples will be set free from the cruel bondage and deadly culture of satan the pretender. The time of the Kingdom of God is upon us. Let His Kingdom come. Let His will be done on Earth as it is in Heaven. Let us live according to His laws and principles. Let His culture reign supreme. Let the Earth be filled with His glory.

(*God's Big Idea*, Chapter Three)

Are you prepared to declare independence from the corrupted world and accept your role as a Kingdom citizen?

The Master Gardener

IN THE BEGINNING WAS THE WORD, AND THE WORD WAS WITH GOD, AND THE WORD WAS GOD. HE WAS WITH GOD IN THE BEGINNING. THROUGH HIM ALL THINGS WERE MADE; WITHOUT HIM NOTHING WAS MADE THAT HAS BEEN MADE (JOHN 1:1–3).

TODAY'S DEVOTION

Although John's reference to the "Word" through whom "all things were made" refers to Jesus Christ, the Son of God, the Spirit of God is also the Spirit of Christ, because they are all of one essence—one God in three Persons. By right and agency of creation, the Holy Spirit was the Master Gardener of Eden, the Governor of God's original colony on Earth. Like human colonial governors, He guides and oversees the lives and welfare of His citizens. Unlike His human counterparts, however, who live in fancy houses and mansions made with human hands, the Governor of the Kingdom lives in the hearts and lives of His citizens. As He was in Eden, He is still the Master Gardener, overseeing the planting, growth, fruitfulness, and reproduction of Kingdom "gardens" in the lives of Kingdom citizens and throughout the world.

(God's Big Idea, Chapter Four)

DAY 13—*The Master Gardener*

1. A well-cared-for garden signals the presence of life in its fullest abundance, vitality, and beauty. What are some ways a garden can become unattractive or dead-looking?

2. The Master Gardener of Eden had been present and intimately involved in its creation. He placed caretakers in the Garden to help tend to it. When they were banished for disobedience, what happened to the Garden?

3. Do you yearn to live in the midst of a beautiful garden created by the Master Gardener? How can you make this happen today?

4. What can you learn from the Master Gardener, the Holy Spirit, about tending to your personal garden of colorful bounty?

5. By right and agency of creation, the Holy Spirit was the Master Gardener of Eden, the Governor of God's original colony on Earth who guides and oversees the lives and welfare of His citizens. Have you accepted His guidance with thankfulness?

MEDITATION

*The Islands of the Bahamas are the home of many beautiful gardens, both public and private. Most Bahamians take great pride in doing everything possible to make our nation a true island paradise of botanical richness and splendor. Of course, the same is true in many other parts of the world. There is something about a garden that stirs an inner chord in the spirit of most of us, a chord of peace, harmony... and **rightness**, as if to say, "This is the way nature is supposed to be." And of course, that is true.*

(*God's Big Idea*, Chapter Four)

What other things stir your inner chord to peace, harmony, and rightness?

Carrying Out the King's Will

YOUR KINGDOM COME, YOUR WILL BE DONE ON EARTH AS IT IS IN HEAVEN (MATTHEW 6:10).

TODAY'S DEVOTION

Carrying out the will of the king is the paramount responsibility of the governor. The big difference between a king and a prime minister or a president is that the last two cannot always have their will or way in the country. They have to negotiate with Parliament or Congress. They have to debate and discuss and often make compromises just to get part of what they want. Even then the final legislation is subject to judicial review and can be overturned if it is judged to violate the constitution.

(*God's Big Idea*, Chapter Four)

DAY 14—*Carrying Out the King's Will*

CONSIDERATIONS

1. God is a God of government, not anarchy. In His orderly assembly of creation, God established His rule of law. How has that rule been distorted by the pretender?

2. What can believers do to restore the Master Gardener's government?

3. Proverbs 29:18 says, "Where there is no revelation, the people cast off restraint; but blessed is he who keeps the law." List a few areas where you have witnessed people casting off restraint.

4. God appointed a Governor, the Holy Spirit, to oversee the overall garden expansion program. Are believers aware of their responsibility to carry out the will of the King through the prompting of the Governor?

5. A kingdom is not a democratic system—in a kingdom, the king's word is law and his will is absolute. Does our 21st-century mindset of independence keep us from submitting to our King's authority?

MEDITATION

The Bible is about a King, His Kingdom, and His royal family. It is a royal document chronicling the purposes, desires, and decrees of the King, as well as the activities, past history, and future destiny of His children and heirs. It also describes the King's expansion program, His plan to expand His heavenly realm into earthly territory.

(*God's Big Idea*, Chapter Four)

How does the concept of being a royal heir conflict or mesh with your concept of being an independent individual?

Our Governor, the Holy Spirit

IN THE SAME WAY, THE SPIRIT HELPS US IN OUR WEAKNESS. WE DO NOT KNOW WHAT WE OUGHT TO PRAY FOR, BUT THE SPIRIT HIMSELF INTERCEDES FOR US WITH GROANS THAT WORDS CANNOT EXPRESS. AND HE WHO SEARCHES OUR HEARTS KNOWS THE MIND OF THE SPIRIT, BECAUSE THE SPIRIT INTERCEDES FOR THE SAINTS IN ACCORDANCE WITH GOD'S WILL (ROMANS 8:26-27).

TODAY'S DEVOTION

Governors in a kingdom are personal appointees of the king. They may be personal friends of the king, or at least known to him by reputation or recommendation. Either way, they are chosen for their loyalty to the king and their commitment to his policies. His purpose is their purpose, and his objectives, their objectives. Quite often they come from the very center of the king's court, intimates of the king who understand his thoughts and are of one mind with him.

This certainly describes the Holy Spirit, who never speaks of His own accord, but only that which He has received from God the Father, the King of Heaven. He is perfectly suited to be Governor of Heaven's Kingdom gardens on Earth because He knows perfectly the heart and mind of the King. This intimacy enables Him to conform the hearts and minds of Kingdom citizens to those of the King, thus shaping the "gardens" of their lives to faithfully manifest the government and culture of Heaven.

(*God's Big Idea*, Chapter Four)

CONSIDERATIONS

1. The better you know a person, the more you can understand the person's motivations and temperament. How well do you know the Governor who was sent to counsel and comfort you?

2. The intimacy that the Governor has with the King enables Him to conform the hearts and minds of Kingdom citizens to those of the King. How does this relationship shape the gardens of their lives to faithfully manifest the government and culture of Heaven?

3. Because the Governor always carries out the will of the King, His presence in us enables us to do the same. In what ways can believers reflect the heart, nature, and character of our King?

4. A governor establishes the authority of a king. Why do you think many people, both inside and outside the Kingdom, are confused about who the Holy Spirit is and what He does?

5. What the Spirit says will always be in agreement with what the Father and the Son say, and with what the Bible, the written Word of God, says. When contradictions are preached, do you immediately go to the Governor for clarification?

MEDITATION

As Governor of the Kingdom, the Holy Spirit is the official designated representative through whom all information from and about the King and His Kingdom passes to His citizens. Because He is in Heaven seated at the right hand of His Father, it is impossible for us to receive any information from Christ, our King, except through the Holy Spirit. The Spirit is the one who guides us into all truth (see John 16:13), teaches us all things, and reminds us of everything Jesus taught us (see John 14:26). As long as the Governor is here, the King is here. As long as the Governor is here, the presence, power, and authority of the King are here. As long as the Governor is here, the Kingdom of Heaven is present on the Earth.

(*God's Big Idea*, Chapter Four)

Do you continually make yourself available for the Governor to speak to you? How can you be more open to receive His guidance?

DAY 16

Fulfilling His Promise

I TELL YOU THE TRUTH, ANYONE WHO HAS FAITH IN ME WILL DO WHAT I HAVE BEEN DOING. HE WILL DO EVEN GREATER THINGS THAN THESE, BECAUSE I AM GOING TO THE FATHER (JOHN 14:12).

TODAY'S DEVOTION

All of our talk about reproducing Kingdom gardens on Earth is simply another way of saying that God is in the process of re-colonizing the planet with His Kingdom government and culture. This mission was so critical that He could entrust it to no one other than His Son, who alone possessed all the necessary qualifications. Jesus came into the world as a government agent on special assignment. Pilate, too, was a government official. This is why he understood Jesus' words when the religious leaders did not; he and Jesus were talking kingdom language. ...

By His own declaration, Jesus did nothing on His own, but only what He saw His Father doing (see John 5:19). And what did Jesus do? He healed the sick, made the lame walk, gave sight to the blind, hearing to the deaf, and speech to the mute. He cast out demons and raised the dead. Jesus did all these things because He saw them first in the mind and heart of His Father. He knew these things were His Father's will, so He did them. The colon was clear. The border between countries was open, and the loving, merciful, compassionate, and healing will of the King passed from His supra-natural realm into the realm of the natural.

(*God's Big Idea*, Chapter Four)

CONSIDERATIONS

1. The word "colony" comes from the Latin word *colonia,* which is transliterated into the Greek as *kolonia.* Literally, it means "cultivate," just as in planting and nurturing a garden. What does colonize mean to you in regard to planting Kingdom gardens?

2. What do *culture, agriculture,* and *horticulture* mean in relation to planting Kingdom gardens?

3. What connection did the Greeks make between the colon and the key to government?

4. When this connection is made from top to bottom, from Heaven to Earth, from the King to His citizens through the link of the Holy Spirit, what is the result?

5. The Governor, Holy Spirit, wants to do the same things in and through us that Jesus did. Are most believers ready and willing to be His instruments of healing and power?

MEDITATION

The Holy Spirit came to dwell in us for the purpose
of fulfilling the promise of John 14:12 in and through us.
Christ is the Head, in Heaven, and we are His Body,
on Earth. The Governor delivers the will of the Head to
the Earth and carries it out through us, the Body. The Master
Gardener takes the seeds and plans of the Owner and transfers
the Garden of His supra-natural realm into the natural world.

(*God's Big Idea*, Chapter Four)

How willing are you to become a useful, pliable, and available instrument for the Creator's plan?

Who Is Tending Your Garden?

No good tree bears bad fruit, nor does a bad tree bear good fruit. Each tree is recognized by its own fruit. People do not pick figs from thornbushes, or grapes from briers. The good man brings good things out of the good stored up in his heart, and the evil man brings evil things out of the evil stored up in his heart. For out of the overflow of his heart his mouth speaks. Why do you call Me, "Lord, Lord," and do not do what I say? (Luke 6:43-46)

TODAY'S DEVOTION

Successful gardens may have many caretakers, but only one master gardener, one person whose vision oversees the overall design. More than one guiding plan leads to confusion, inefficiency, inconsistent results, and stunted fruitfulness. This is precisely the dilemma many believers face. On the one hand, they claim to follow the King and to live according to His government, while on the other they continue to listen to the desires of the pretender and fail or refuse to uproot the "weeds" of evil, rebellion, and destruction he has sown in their hearts. And then they wonder why their garden is choked off and produces little fruit.

Successful gardens may have many caretakers, but only one master gardener, one person whose vision oversees the overall design. More than one guiding plan leads to confusion, inefficiency, inconsistent results, and stunted fruitfulness. This is precisely the dilemma many believers face.

(*God's Big Idea*, Chapter Five)

DAY 17—*Who Is Tending Your Garden?*

CONSIDERATIONS

1. If believers listen to the desires of the pretender and fail or refuse to uproot the "weeds" of evil, rebellion, and destruction he has sown in their hearts, what is the inevitable result?

2. Gardens are known by the consistency, quality, and abundance of the fruit they produce, and these are direct reflections of the skill and character of the gardener. If the garden is nonproducing, is this a reflection of the gardener as well?

3. The quality of the fruit depends on the nature of the root. In other words, the fruit we bear in our lives reveals who is tending our garden— the Master Gardener or the pretender. Who is tending your garden?

4. Because the natural reflects the supernatural, the human race has mistreated the planet and misused its resources, which is a representation of the spiritual devastation wrought by the pretender's depraved rule. List a few examples of this mistreatment or misuse.

5. Every day we make choices that determine which fruit will manifest in our lives—either the bad fruit of the pretender or the good fruit of the Master Gardener. How easy is it for you to make the hard choices that produce the good fruit?

DAY 17—*Who Is Tending Your Garden?*

MEDITATION

The Bible is the record of God's plan to reclaim the earthly dominion and restore it to His original design and intent. As we have already seen, God's big idea from the beginning was to extend His heavenly Kingdom to Earth, and He chose to do it through His very own children. This was not a religious act but an act of state. Adam and Eve had no religion in the Garden of Eden. What they did have was continuing fellowship with their Creator as they ruled the created order as His vice regents. In bringing Heaven to Earth, the King was simply enacting His own governmental policy. His purpose was to fill the Earth with His glory. He wanted to bring His own nature to the Earth, and that nature was reflected in the lush beauty, abundant fruitfulness, and absolute perfection of the Garden.

(*God's Big Idea*, Chapter Five)

Who is tending your garden?

Seeking and Saving the Lost

Jesus said to him, "Today salvation has come to this house, because this man, too, is a son of Abraham. For the Son of Man came to seek and to save what was lost" (Luke 19:8-10).

TODAY'S DEVOTION

It was not God's purpose, however, to leave Heaven and come to the Earth to rule it directly. He chose instead to give rulership of this domain to beings specially created for it. God created human beings specifically for the purpose of dominating the Earth for Him and filling it with His nature, character, and culture. No other created beings in Heaven or on Earth were suited for the task. Only humans were fit to rule the Earth because that is the way God designed us. ...

Unfortunately, in an act of treason and betrayal, the first two humans inadvertently surrendered their kingdom to one who greatly desired it but who was not qualified to rule it. ...

Jesus Christ, the King's Son, came to Earth to take it back. He came to regain what was lost. When Jesus announced the arrival of the Kingdom of Heaven in Matthew 4:17, He was not bringing anything new to the Earth. He was bringing back what man had lost, and what the pretender had stolen.

(God's Big Idea, Chapter Five)

CONSIDERATIONS

1. What happened that caused a demonic pretender to ascend the throne and the earthly realm to declare its independence from Heaven?

2. Zacchaeus was despised because of his unethical financial practices. How was his life changed after an encounter with Jesus? Compare Zacchaeus with a modern-day person fitting his description.

3. *"For the Son of Man came to seek and to save what was lost"* (Luke 19:10). Notice that Jesus said He came "to seek and to save what was lost," rather than "who" was lost. Other versions of the Bible translate the phrase, *"that which was lost."* How do you explain this distinction?

4. In Luke 19:10, Jesus was referring also to the Kingdom of Heaven itself, which had been lost, and which He came to seek and to save. In what ways has the Kingdom been found and redeemed?

5. In what ways has the Kingdom remained lost and unredeemed?

MEDITATION

People everywhere are looking desperately for the Kingdom, even if they don't know it. This is why, when they encounter it—when they hear the message of the Kingdom—they, like Zacchaeus, find it irresistible. It is this attractive, magnetic quality of the Kingdom that Jesus had in mind when He said, "From the days of John the Baptist until now, the kingdom of heaven has been forcefully advancing, and forceful men lay hold of it" (Matt. 11:12). Once people know about the Kingdom and understand it, they flock to it, desperate to enter. This is only natural. The Kingdom is what we were created for.

(*God's Big Idea*, Chapter Five)

It is natural to want to be part of the Kingdom—why do some resist?

Self-government Disasters

On the evening of that first day of the week, when the disciples were together, with the doors locked for fear of the Jews, Jesus came and stood among them and said, "Peace be with you!" After He said this, He showed them His hands and side. The disciples were overjoyed when they saw the Lord.

Again Jesus said, "Peace be with you! As the Father has sent Me, I am sending you." And with that He breathed on them and said, "Receive the Holy Spirit. If you forgive anyone his sins, they are forgiven; if you do not forgive them, they are not forgiven" (John 20:19-23).

TODAY'S DEVOTION

When Adam and Eve declared independence in the Garden by disobeying God's one restriction, they thought they could govern themselves and their earthly domain at least as well as God could, if not better. They were wrong. No sooner had they "freed" themselves from God's control than they found themselves deposed from their earthly thrones altogether. Their sin against God corrupted their human nature, and they became enslaved to the power and will of the pretender. He preferred to work behind the scenes, however, pulling the strings while letting them think they were governing themselves.

Humanity's efforts at self-government have been disastrous from the beginning. ...The first act of human self-government after leaving Eden was an act of fratricide: Cain murdered his brother Abel. And as a race we humans have been chained by envy, hatred, and murder ever since.

(*God's Big Idea*, Chapter Five)

CONSIDERATIONS

1. Rather than bringing about self-improvement, all our efforts at self-government have moved us closer and closer to self-destruction. Why?

2. Thousands of wars and six millennia of social, scientific, and technological advancement have not changed things to any great degree. Why?

3. Jesus Christ inaugurated His public mission by announcing the return of the Kingdom and calling people to respond: "Repent, for the kingdom of heaven is near" (Matt. 4:17b). The word *repent* is seldom heard in today's political, religious, or other conversations. Why is there a need for an understanding of this concept?

4. For 33 years, from Jesus' birth to His ascension, the Holy Spirit showed up nowhere on the Earth except in Jesus Himself. Why are believers now worthy vessels for the indwelling of the Holy Spirit?

5. Through His death and resurrection Jesus cleansed us of our sin—our rebellion against God—and gave us access to His Kingdom. Why is it so easy for believers to want to self-govern? What keeps us from submitting totally to His authority?

MEDITATION

[God] gave us the Governor to teach us how
to live as Kingdom citizens. The Governor, the
Holy Spirit, is the Master Gardener who ensures
that the gardens of our lives produce good fruit that
is appropriate and pleasing to the King, to whom
the gardens belong. Could there be any greater
freedom—or any greater destiny—than this?

(*God's Big Idea*, Chapter Five)

Is your independent nature stronger than your submissive nature? What can you do to surrender your idea and accept God's big idea?

Illegal Resident

IN THE SAME WAY, COUNT YOURSELVES DEAD TO SIN BUT ALIVE TO GOD IN CHRIST JESUS. THEREFORE DO NOT LET SIN REIGN IN YOUR MORTAL BODY SO THAT YOU OBEY ITS EVIL DESIRES. DO NOT OFFER THE PARTS OF YOUR BODY TO SIN, AS INSTRUMENTS OF WICKEDNESS, BUT RATHER OFFER YOURSELVES TO GOD, AS THOSE WHO HAVE BEEN BROUGHT FROM DEATH TO LIFE; AND OFFER THE PARTS OF YOUR BODY TO HIM AS INSTRUMENTS OF RIGHTEOUSNESS. FOR SIN SHALL NOT BE YOUR MASTER, BECAUSE YOU ARE NOT UNDER LAW, BUT UNDER GRACE.

…YOU HAVE BEEN SET FREE FROM SIN AND HAVE BECOME SLAVES TO RIGHTEOUSNESS.…

BUT NOW THAT YOU HAVE BEEN SET FREE FROM SIN AND HAVE BECOME SLAVES TO GOD, THE BENEFIT YOU REAP LEADS TO HOLINESS, AND THE RESULT IS ETERNAL LIFE. FOR THE WAGES OF SIN IS DEATH, BUT THE GIFT OF GOD IS ETERNAL LIFE IN CHRIST JESUS OUR LORD (ROMANS 6:11-14,18,22-23).

TODAY'S DEVOTION

We were created to be filled with the Spirit of God and to live in perfect harmony and fellowship with Him, not to be under the thumb of a demonic pretender exercising illegitimate authority. This is why whenever Jesus encountered a demonic spirit possessing a human being, He cast out the spirit as an illegal resident. As believers, we have a choice as to who we allow to tend our garden. One choice leads to a wasted and unfulfilled life while the other leads to great abundance and fullness of life. ...

We have been trained by religion to be scared of the devil. Most of our churches have taught us to regard the world situation as hopeless, to prepare ourselves to leave, and then to pray for the Lord to rescue us out of this world. Having conceded victory to the pretender, we feel that all we can hope to do is circle the wagons and defend ourselves as best we can until Christ comes back and takes us away. We have become a bunch of holy sissies.

(God's Big Idea, Chapter Five)

DAY 20—*Illegal Resident*

CONSIDERATIONS

1. The devil wants to take up residence in us through demonic powers because he knows that once he is inside he can work through us to:

   _____

   _____

   _____

   _____

   _____ .

2. *"My prayer is not that You take them out of the world but that You protect them from the evil one"* (John 17:15). Why do you think Jesus felt it necessary to pray this prayer to God for us?

3. Why is it so hard for believers to realize that, ultimately, satan the pretender poses no threat?

4. In league with our King, we have more power and authority than any fallen angel could ever hope to have. Is this the mindset of most believers? Why?

5. Our protection from the evil one is certain because of the King's love for us. List several times when you know your King has averted you from danger, or has forewarned you about a problem or situation.

MEDITATION

*We are the legal rulers on Earth with the power,
authority, and protection of our King behind us. Satan
is a liar, usurper, and pretender whose illegal power
over us was broken forever at the Cross. Although
we must always be on our guard against his schemes,
deception, and treachery, as Kingdom citizens exercising
our legitimate authority, we have no reason to fear him.*

(*God's Big Idea*, Chapter Five)

Has the illegal resident taken up space in your community, school, house, heart?

Boot him out today!

Kingdom Influence

ONCE, HAVING BEEN ASKED BY THE PHARISEES WHEN THE KINGDOM OF GOD WOULD COME, JESUS REPLIED, "THE KINGDOM OF GOD DOES NOT COME WITH YOUR CAREFUL OBSERVATION, NOR WILL PEOPLE SAY, 'HERE IT IS,' OR 'THERE IT IS,' **BECAUSE THE KINGDOM OF GOD IS WITHIN YOU**" (LUKE 17:20-21).

TODAY'S DEVOTION

By now it should be abundantly clear that the Kingdom of Heaven is not a religion and has nothing at all to do with religion. In Eden, the original Kingdom Garden on Earth, there was no religion. There was no "worship" in the sense that we usually understand the word. Adam and Eve enjoyed full, open, and transparent fellowship and interaction with their Creator in a mutual relationship of pure love with absolutely no guilt, shame, or fear. Their disobedience broke that relationship, and humanity's efforts to restore it on their own without divine assistance gave rise to religion.

The Kingdom of Heaven is the sovereign rulership of the King (God) over a territory (Earth), impacting it with His will, purposes, and intent, producing a citizenry of people (*ekklesia*—the church) who express a culture reflecting the nature and lifestyle of the King. Therefore, as we have already seen, the Kingdom of Heaven is a real, literal country, although invisible to physical eyes because it is spiritual in nature. As King of Heaven, God's big idea was to extend the influence of His heavenly country over and throughout the Earth. So we are really talking about two things here: God's country and its influence.

(*God's Big Idea*, Chapter Six)

CONSIDERATIONS

1. Wherever the Kingdom of God is, the Kingdom of Heaven has influence. So wherever we go as Kingdom citizens, the influence of the King should go along. Are believers as aware as they should be about their sphere of influence?

2. A strong and rich culture can wield influence far beyond its geographical boundaries. Name a few ways culture or values have infiltrated nations outside their origin.

3. There are two kinds of influence: the influence of the moment, which spreads rapidly and then disappears just as quickly; and lasting influence, which grows more slowly, but succeeds through persistence and permeation. Give examples of how both types of influence can or cannot be of value to planting gardens for His glory.

4. What is meant by the term "Irresistible Influence" concerning the Kingdom?

5. At least 4,000 years have passed from the time Adam and Eve lost the Kingdom in Eden until Christ announced its return. God has been continually working out His plan. Do you see an end in sight?

MEDITATION

*Ultimately, the influence of God's Kingdom is irresistible. This does not mean that everyone eventually will enter the Kingdom, but it does mean that someday everyone will acknowledge the reality, authority, and absolute supremacy of the Kingdom of Heaven. The apostle Paul stated plainly that the day will come when "at the name of Jesus every knee should bow, in heaven and on earth and under the earth, and every tongue confess that Jesus Christ is Lord, to the glory of God the Father" (Phil. 2:10-11). The word **Lord** means "owner," and is a term properly applied to a king. Christ is the King of an eternal, all-powerful, all-knowing, present-everywhere Kingdom, and one day everyone will confess that this is so, even those who have rejected His Kingdom.*

(*God's Big Idea*, Chapter Six)

Is your influence making a difference in those around you? In those you love?

Expanding Your Influence Through Prayer

... THE KINGDOM OF HEAVEN IS LIKE A MUS-
TARD SEED, WHICH A MAN TOOK AND
PLANTED IN HIS FIELD. THOUGH IT IS THE SMALLEST
OF ALL YOUR SEEDS, YET WHEN IT GROWS, IT IS THE
LARGEST OF GARDEN PLANTS AND BECOMES A TREE,
SO THAT THE BIRDS OF THE AIR COME AND PERCH IN
ITS BRANCHES (MATTHEW 13:31-32).

TODAY'S DEVOTION

Anyone who spends any amount of time in the kitchen knows what yeast is and what it does (knowing *how* it does what it does is another matter). Yeast is one of the most powerful influencing agents in the world, and it exists for one reason: to infect whatever it is mixed into with its presence and influence. Jesus' comparison of the Kingdom of Heaven to yeast makes us think right away about impact.

While people caught up in religion think about leaving the Earth, Kingdom citizens focus on transforming it, the way yeast transforms a batch of dough. Yeast is not about giving up or giving in. It is about taking over. Yeast does not abandon dough; it affects it. Yeast never becomes dough. Instead, dough becomes yeast. Dough is weaker than yeast, and as the yeast works its way through, the dough gradually but irresistibly takes on the characteristics of the yeast.

(God's Big Idea, Chapter Six)

CONSIDERATIONS

1. Yeast has not finished its job until it has "worked all through the dough." In the same way, Christ is not coming back to an Earth that is not "worked all through" with the influence of His Kingdom. Believers may feel frustrated because of an apparent lack of progress—but what does Christ say?

2. For many believers, prayer does not work the way it should because they have made it a religious exercise of pleading for a favor rather than a legal act of asserting their rights and privileges as Kingdom citizens. How do you view prayer? Is it working for you?

3. Becoming a Kingdom citizen through faith in Christ and through the cleansing of our sins by His blood gives us complete access to these three gifts:

4. When we petition the King properly, we are asking for what He has already promised. According to Hebrews 4:16, we can approach the throne of grace with _____, so that we may receive _____ and find _____ to help in our time of need.

5. Write the Lord's Prayer and examine each word as you write.

MEDITATION

*First, He says, we must address our petition to the right
Person: "Our Father in heaven…." God the Father is the
King who is ruling in Heaven, and we are His citizens in His
Garden outpost on Earth who are petitioning for an audience.*

*Second, we must pay proper respect when addressing the King:
"…hallowed be Your name…." To hallow God's name means
to render utmost respect and reverence to His name, because His
name is identified with His reputation. And because God is very
jealous of His reputation, He is also jealous of His name. …*

*Third, our petition should always reflect not our own will,
but the will of the King, for the will of the King is law:
"…Your kingdom come, Your will be done on earth as it is
in heaven…." Remember, this is Jesus instructing His disciples
to pray. In other words, the King Himself is telling us what
to ask Him for. He says nothing about cars or clothes or food.
Instead, He says, "Petition for My government influence to
come to Earth, for My intentions, purposes, culture, lifestyle,
and will to be done on Earth just as they are in Heaven."*

(*God's Big Idea*, Chapter Six)

Prayerfully and deliberately say the Lord's Prayer
aloud to your God and King.

Praying for Yeast

BUT SEEK FIRST *[GOD'S]* KINGDOM AND *[GOD'S]* RIGHTEOUSNESS, AND ALL THESE THINGS WILL BE GIVEN TO YOU AS WELL (MATTHEW 6:33).

TODAY'S DEVOTION

I f you are one of those people who have trouble praying because you never know what to pray for, I have just destroyed your last excuse. You don't have to pray long as long as you pray right. Take the time every day—at your bedside when you first get up, while in the shower, while getting dressed, while driving to work, or whatever—to pray simply, "Lord, let Your Kingdom come and let Your will be done in my life today as it is in Heaven." Start praying that prayer, and look for opportunities that God gives you for fulfilling it. Tend to God's business this way, and watch how He starts tending to yours.

Even Jesus' prayer for His followers in John chapter 17 is a "yeast" prayer:

> *My prayer is not that You take them out of the world but that You protect them from the evil one. They are not of the world, even as I am not of it. Sanctify them by the truth; Your word is truth. As You sent Me into the world, I have sent them into the world"* (John 17:15-18).

(*God's Big Idea*, Chapter Six)

CONSIDERATIONS

1. When we focus our hearts and minds to pray for Heaven to come to Earth, then the next part of Jesus' Garden expansion prayer makes more sense: *"Give us today our daily bread"* (Matt. 6:11). What connection can you draw from this statement?

2. "Daily bread" certainly refers to food, but also the ancient Jews often used the word *bread* as an idiom that meant everything necessary for life. Do today's believers need more than physical nourishment when confronting challenges? Explain.

3. How can the yeast of His influence help us bring about His Kingdom expansion on Earth?

4. What are several differences between saying, "I am in business for myself for my own profit," and saying, "I am in His business for His influence."

5. We are not here to *escape*; we are here to *reshape*. Are there times when believers should take a stand about issues, circumstances, injustice? List a few.

MEDITATION

Many believers say, "I want a Christian job with a Christian boss in a Christian workplace." While there certainly are believers whom the Lord has called to such positions, He calls most of us to bloom and prosper right where we are, in the middle of the finance field, or the hotel field, or the food industry, or education, or government, because there is a whole lot of dough out there with a whole lot of needs. He wants us to infect the hospitality industry, banking, business, politics, sports.

(*God's Big Idea*, Chapter Six)

Are believers effectively infecting their workplaces, communities, and families, with the Kingdom?

Priceless Treasure

THE KINGDOM OF HEAVEN IS LIKE TREASURE HIDDEN IN A FIELD. WHEN A MAN FOUND IT, HE HID IT AGAIN, AND THEN IN HIS JOY WENT AND SOLD ALL HE HAD AND BOUGHT THAT FIELD.

AGAIN, THE KINGDOM OF HEAVEN IS LIKE A MERCHANT LOOKING FOR FINE PEARLS. WHEN HE FOUND ONE OF GREAT VALUE, HE WENT AWAY AND SOLD EVERYTHING HE HAD AND BOUGHT IT (MATTHEW 13:44-46).

TODAY'S DEVOTION

These parables speak of two different types of people and their responses to the Kingdom. The man in the first parable is like most of the people in the world, either searching aimlessly for they know not what, or simply going through life unaware of the priceless treasure at their feet until they stumble upon it (seemingly) by accident. This man may have heard a rumor of treasure in the field and gone looking for it, or he may simply have been crossing the field and come upon the treasure unexpectedly. Either way, the moment he found it, he knew it was what he had been seeking all his life. He immediately recognized its priceless value, and that it was worth any price he had to pay to obtain it. Accordingly, he sold everything he had and bought the field. The Kingdom of Heaven is far more valuable than anything this world has to offer.

In the second parable, the merchant knew what he was looking for: fine pearls. Finding one of "great value," he knew right away that in beauty and worth it far outstripped any other pearl he had ever found, and he too sold everything he had in order to buy it.

Many people know they are searching for something, for some sense of meaning and purpose to life, and some even have at least a vague idea of what they want. They sample different religions, try out various philosophies, and comb through the world's wisdom literature looking for answers and searching for truth. Upon discovering the Kingdom (or being discovered by it), they know intuitively that here, finally, is the answer to all their questions and the end of their long quest.

(*God's Big Idea*, Chapter Six)

CONSIDERATIONS

1. In the two examples cited in Today's Devotion, which person do you more readily identify with? Why?

2. Although the Kingdom gives us access to all the riches of Heaven and all the resources of eternity, some people refuse to accept His free gifts. Why?

3. Entrance into the Kingdom of Heaven is open to all. The King excludes no one from His invitation to possess the priceless treasure. List several Scripture passages that confirm these statements.

4. The invigorating waters of Kingdom life are offered to all without cost or exclusion, yet there will be many who exclude themselves by refusing to drink. Why?

5. God wants to invade Earth with Heaven, to infect Earth with Heaven's culture until Earth begins to look just like Heaven. How will He accomplish His plan?

MEDITATION

The ultimate power and goal of Garden influence is to develop a heavenly culture on Earth that produces a Kingdom community. God wants to invade Earth with Heaven, to infect Earth with Heaven's culture until Earth begins to look just like Heaven. His desire is to build a heavenly community on Earth through the cultivation of His Kingdom culture here. This is both the prayer of Jesus: "Your kingdom come, Your will be done on earth as it is in heaven" (Matt. 6:10), and the plan of God from the beginning: "Let Us make man in Our image…and let them rule…" (Gen. 1:26).

God doesn't want a religion. He doesn't want a weekend ceremony. He isn't looking for a group of weird people dressed in weird clothes saying weird things. God wants a holy community of whole and complete citizens, a community that represents and reflects Heaven on Earth, and He wants to do it through cultivating His Kingdom's culture on Earth through the lives and influence of His people.

(*God's Big Idea*, Chapter Six)

How committed are you to possessing the priceless treasure for your very own?

Pride and Independence

...SIN ENTERED THE WORLD THROUGH ONE MAN, AND DEATH THROUGH SIN, AND IN THIS WAY DEATH CAME TO ALL MEN, BECAUSE ALL SINNED. ...CONSEQUENTLY, JUST AS THE RESULT OF ONE TRESPASS WAS CONDEMNATION FOR ALL MEN, SO ALSO THE RESULT OF ONE ACT OF RIGHTEOUS-NESS WAS JUSTIFICATION THAT BRINGS LIFE FOR ALL MEN. FOR JUST AS THROUGH THE DISOBEDIENCE OF THE ONE MAN THE MANY WERE MADE SINNERS, SO ALSO THROUGH THE OBEDIENCE OF THE ONE MAN THE MANY WILL BE MADE RIGHTEOUS (ROMANS 5:12,18-19).

TODAY'S DEVOTION

Human history has demonstrated time and time again that as a race we are manifestly incapable of governing ourselves effectively apart from the Spirit and principles of God. God, of course, knew this from the start, which is why, in the wake of man's rebellion, He set into motion His plan to reclaim, or re-colonize the planet, a plan He established even before the foundations of the Earth were laid.

Re-colonization is an unfamiliar concept because it is extremely rare for a colony, once it has declared its independence from a kingdom, to later change its mind and desire to return to colonial status. God, however, initiated the re-colonization of Earth for two reasons: because His sovereign will and intent will never be thwarted, and because our survival as a race depends on it.

(*God's Big Idea*, Chapter Seven)

CONSIDERATIONS

1. A king is the governing authority over a territory impacting it with his will, purpose, and intent, producing a citizenry of people who reflect the king's morals, values, and lifestyle. What are the differences between a republic and a kingdom?

2. Why is living in a kingdom much more challenging than living in a democracy?

3. How is individuality looked upon in a kingdom? A democracy?

4. Why did God give Adam and Eve free will if He knew they would disobey Him?

5. Rebelling against the Kingdom is sin; sins are the day-to-day actions that constitute rebel-like behavior. How can believers stymie the rebellious nature within?

MEDITATION

This personal independence is the number one tenet of capitalism and democratic republics. The thing God hates is the very thing we magnify. The thing that God says is our condemnation is the very thing we regard as our highest achievement. As independent individuals we can do whatever we like and pursue our own happiness and our own joy at our own expense. We take great pride in "doing our own thing," while God says, "That's the very problem with the world." It's a paradox. This is why it is very difficult to live in the Kingdom of God and live at the same time in a democracy under a capitalistic system. It is hard to strike a balance between the two because the principles that operate them are diametrically opposed to each other.

(*God's Big Idea*, Chapter Seven)

Is your sense of pride and independence holding you back from receiving all that God has for you?

"Bring Them Here to Me"

JESUS REPLIED, "THEY DO NOT NEED TO GO AWAY. YOU GIVE THEM SOMETHING TO EAT."

"WE HAVE HERE ONLY FIVE LOAVES OF BREAD AND TWO FISH," THEY ANSWERED.

"BRING THEM HERE TO ME," HE SAID. AND HE DIRECTED THE PEOPLE TO SIT DOWN ON THE GRASS. TAKING THE FIVE LOAVES AND THE TWO FISH AND LOOKING UP TO HEAVEN, HE GAVE THANKS AND BROKE THE LOAVES. THEN HE GAVE THEM TO THE DISCIPLES, AND THE DISCIPLES GAVE THEM TO THE PEOPLE. THEY ALL ATE AND WERE SATISFIED, AND THE DISCIPLES PICKED UP TWELVE BASKETFULS OF BROKEN PIECES THAT WERE LEFT OVER. THE NUMBER OF THOSE WHO ATE WAS ABOUT FIVE THOUSAND MEN, BESIDES WOMEN AND CHILDREN (MATTHEW 14:16-21).

TODAY'S DEVOTION

Culture reflects government. In the world's culture, some people go hungry. Some people are poor or sick or lacking some of the basic necessities for high quality of life. Inequities abound and injustice is rampant. Not in Kingdom culture. Wherever Jesus went, sick people were made well—because there is no sickness in the Kingdom. Hungry people were fed and satisfied—because there is no hunger or lack of any kind in the Kingdom.

When 5,000 people in a remote place needed to be fed, Jesus did the natural thing (from the Kingdom perspective)—He fed them. His disciples wanted to send the people away to buy food because they were approaching the situation from a point of view of lack. Jesus, however, knew there was no lack because He had unlimited access to the unlimited resources of His Father's Kingdom.

When Jesus took those five loaves and two fish from His disciples, He took them out of capitalism and into Kingdom-ism. Once inside that new economy, the very atoms in that fish and bread began to behave differently. ...What we call a miracle was simply normal activity in the Kingdom. And it should be normal activity for all who manifest Kingdom culture.

(God's Big Idea, Chapter Seven)

CONSIDERATIONS

1. When Kingdom living prevails, things such as hunger, fear, discouragement, defeat, curses, and greed do not exist. List other maladies that do not exist in Heaven's culture on Earth.

2. Jesus' disciples struggled when learning how to shift their thinking and their behavior from the worldly culture of their birth to the Kingdom culture. What is one of the most difficult behaviors you have had to shift your thinking about? Have you been successful?

3. Jesus challenges our behavior, beliefs, values, thoughts, perceptions, assumptions, and expectations. Only through the power of the Holy Spirit can believers change worldly culture traditions. True or False? Why?

4. As there are various Chinatown subcultures within larger city cultures, have you built a Kingdom subculture within your larger workplace or neighborhood culture?

5. Are believers worldwide receiving the kind of attention that Jesus prompted when He was spreading Kingdom culture? Why or why not?

MEDITATION

In the same way, people should be able to walk into our presence or our homes or our churches and feel like they have walked into another country. They should be able to tell immediately by our language, dress, manners, attitude, and behavior that we are not of this world. Our culture should stand out so clearly that no one can mistake it.

Life with Jesus was always this way, which is why He attracted so much attention. People either loved Him or hated Him, accepted Him or rejected Him, but no one ignored Him. Everywhere He went He brought Kingdom culture. Throngs of people surrounded Him because He showed them the power, quality, nature, and irresistible appeal of a culture that could make them victors in life rather than victims—and then He told them how to get it.

(*God's Big Idea*, Chapter Seven)

Jesus caused a commotion wherever He went. Are you stirring up reactions by taking Kingdom culture to your school, workplace, church?

Culture Revelations (Part 1)

[J*ESUS SAYS*], "YOU HAVE HEARD THAT IT WAS SAID, 'LOVE YOUR NEIGHBOR AND HATE YOUR ENEMY.' BUT I TELL YOU: LOVE YOUR ENEMIES AND PRAY FOR THOSE WHO PERSECUTE YOU, THAT YOU MAY BE SONS OF YOUR FATHER IN HEAVEN" (MATTHEW 5:38–45A).

I n addition, culture is the total life of a people passed on to their descendants. Culture is an extremely powerful thing. Its roots grow deep and its influence reaches far. This is why a group of people bound together by culture can live for generations in a country not their own and still maintain their distinct identity. Culture encompasses the totality of life: dress, food, drink, customs, manners, etiquette, protocol, attitudes toward children and the elderly, religious beliefs, ethical and moral values, social norms, and both public and private behavior.

If we are manifesting Kingdom culture in our lives, people who meet us should be able to say, "I think I just entered Heaven. You don't lie, you don't cheat, you don't steal, you don't sleep around, you've been married to the same person for thirty years; what's up with you? Where are you from? Why are you so different?" When people outside the Kingdom look at Kingdom citizens or a Kingdom community, they should see a culture distinctly different—and much more attractive—than their own.

(*God's Big Idea*, Chapter Seven)

CONSIDERATIONS

Culture reveals itself in at least 16 specific ways. Write a short definition for the following eight, applying them to your personal experiences:

Values:

Priorities:

Behaviors:

Standards:

Celebrations:

Morality:

Relationships:

Ethics:

MEDITATION

The character of a nation's culture is revealed also in the ethical standards it practices. These may be quite different from the "official" standards established by law for ethical behavior. Many corrupt and unethical governments have given lip service to the highest ethical standards even as their leaders victimized the people and plundered the treasury for their own enrichment. Corruption as the moral fabric of a culture guarantees the poverty of a nation, not only economically, but morally and spiritually as well.

(*God's Big Idea*, Chapter Seven)

How has defining these eight characteristics of culture expanded your view of Kingdom culture?

DAY 28

Culture Revelations (Part 2)

MAKE SURE THAT NOBODY PAYS BACK WRONG FOR WRONG, BUT ALWAYS TRY TO BE KIND TO EACH OTHER AND TO EVERYONE ELSE. BE JOYFUL ALWAYS; PRAY CONTINUALLY; GIVE THANKS IN ALL CIRCUMSTANCES, FOR THIS IS GOD'S WILL FOR YOU IN CHRIST JESUS. DO NOT PUT OUT THE SPIRIT'S FIRE; DO NOT TREAT PROPHECIES WITH CONTEMPT. TEST EVERYTHING. HOLD ONTO THE GOOD. AVOID EVERY KIND OF EVIL (1 THESSALONIANS 5:15-22).

TODAY'S DEVOTION

Culture reveals itself also in the attitude of the people. There are certain countries you can visit where the people are very warm and friendly, who are appreciative of visitors and go out of their way to make them feel welcome. I love visiting places like that. At the other end of the spectrum are those countries where the people in general are rude, or arrogant, or superior in their demeanor, where even people in the "service" industries such as hotels and restaurants act as though they are insulted by your presence and that they are doing you a favor by serving you.

No one should ever feel unwelcome when they enter a place where Kingdom culture is present. On the contrary, they should feel as though they have entered Heaven itself. This is why the Bible says, "Let love prevail among you." That is the culture of Heaven. "Let forgiveness prevail among you." That is the culture of Heaven. "Let joy unspeakable prevail among you." That is the culture of Heaven. "Let the peace that passes understanding prevail among you." That is the culture of Heaven.

(*God's Big Idea*, Chapter Seven)

CONSIDERATIONS

As mentioned yesterday, culture reveals itself in at least 16 specific ways. Write a short definition for the following eight, applying them to your personal experiences:

Social norms:

Attitudes:

Dress:

Food:

Responses:

Drink:

Whatever is permitted:

Whatever is accepted:

MEDITATION

Community means, essentially, that individuality is gone and everybody lives and works for the good of everybody else. Western society, with its emphasis on independence and individualism, has largely lost touch with the concept of community, and this has affected many churches and believers. The time has come for Kingdom citizens to rediscover and reclaim community as an essential part of Kingdom life that is critical to the successful reproduction of Kingdom gardens throughout the Earth. After all, a Kingdom community is a Kingdom garden.

(*God's Big Idea*, Chapter Seven)

How has defining these eight characteristics of culture expanded your view of Kingdom culture?

DAY 29

Dreaming

"FOR MY THOUGHTS ARE NOT YOUR THOUGHTS, NEITHER ARE YOUR WAYS MY WAYS," DECLARES THE LORD. "AS THE HEAVENS ARE HIGHER THAN THE EARTH, SO ARE MY WAYS HIGHER THAN YOUR WAYS AND MY THOUGHTS THAN YOUR THOUGHTS" (ISAIAH 55:8-9).

TODAY'S DEVOTION

I have a dream that before I die I will see and be part of a dynamic, growing community of people among whom there is no sickness, no poverty, and no want. Everyone will be debt free. Depression, worry, and despair will be unknown, every marriage will be strong, successful, and happy, and all the children will respect their parents and live completely free of fear. The entire community will worship the Lord in perfect unity and harmony and with a single common vision.

People from outside will be amazed at what they see. "Do you mean that out of these 50,000 people, nobody is divorced? Why not?"

"Because in our community we don't believe in that. We believe in fixing things up, in repenting, reconciling, and forgiving. That's our nature, our culture."

"Do you mean to tell me that among these 200,000 people there is no incest? How can this be?"

"Because in our community such a thing is detestable. We love our children. They are made in God's image and we care for and protect them. That's our culture."

"Do you mean to tell me that out of half a million people, nobody tells lies?"

"It's true. Lying is unheard of in our community. Truth is our currency. In our community, truth is not the best policy—it is the only policy.

I dream of the day when this will be reality. Fantasy, you say? Utopia? No, simply Kingdom culture in action.

(*God's Big Idea,* Chapter Eight)

CONSIDERATIONS

1. We dream of Heaven because we can't find the community we want here on Earth. Describe a few life circumstances that make believers dream of Heaven rather than face situations.

2. Why is the concept of Heaven on Earth so hard to accept?

3. What will it take for believers to stop dreaming about Heaven and embrace a Kingdom mindset?

4. God's purpose has always been to build a heavenly community on Earth, a community that would reflect in the physical realm the: _____ , _____ , _____ , _____ , and _____ and _____ character of His Kingdom in the spiritual realm.

5. The word *community* comes from the words "common unity," and refers to a group of people who share a common language, food, dress, lifestyle, customs, values, and morals. Name a few commonalities that bind your neighborhood or church together.

MEDITATION

Our assignment as Kingdom citizens and ambassadors is to learn—and then teach others—how to apply the Kingdom to business and bodily health; to single life, marriage, and parenting; to investments and speech; to relationships and professions; to government and media. We have to reintroduce the precepts of the Kingdom of Heaven, the values, morals, principles, and standards by which our society is supposed to live. God's plan, then, is not—and never has been—to establish a religious institution, but to build a living, breathing, and thriving community that reveals to the world what He is like as well as the quality of life under His government.

(*God's Big Idea*, Chapter Eight)

Dreaming about Heaven isn't wrong, but living for God's glory now within the Kingdom of Heaven is His desire for us. Are you dreaming or living?

Reflected Glory

When the queen of Sheba heard about the fame of Solomon and his relation to the name of the Lord, she came to test him with hard questions. Arriving at Jerusalem with a very great caravan—with camels carrying spices, large quantities of gold, and precious stones—she came to Solomon and talked with him about all that she had on her mind. Solomon answered all her questions; nothing was too hard for the king to explain to her. She said to the king, "The report I heard in my own country about your achievements and your wisdom is true. But I did not believe these things until I came and saw them with my own eyes. Indeed, not even half was told me; in wisdom and wealth you have far exceeded the report I heard" (1 Kings 10:1-3,6-7).

TODAY'S DEVOTION

The purpose behind a Kingdom community is to reflect the greatness and glory of the King. Citizens of the community are under the rule of the King and come to manifest His nature. In other words, the people take on the characteristics of the King, display the qualities of the King, and exhibit the culture of the King. As a matter of fact, the quality and nature of any kingdom can be recognized first not by the presence of the king but by the lifestyle of his citizens. Seeing how the people in a kingdom live reveals a great deal about their king.

That's how kingdoms work. Kingdoms are manifested in the culture of the people. So the quality of the community is a manifestation or reflection of the quality of the king.

(*God's Big Idea*, Chapter Eight)

CONSIDERATIONS

1. In your opinion, are the believers in the Western world reflective of God's glory? Why or why not?

2. What are five steps that believers can take to reflect better the glory of God's love and tender mercy?

3. What does your reputation say about your role as a child of the King? Do people immediately know that you are not of this world?

4. "When you are born into wealth, you don't talk about wealth. God's ultimate goal is to bring that kind of life on Earth." Why is it hard for believers to accept the wealth of the Kingdom that God freely offers to them?

5. What is the difference between living within walls of latex and walls of gold?

MEDITATION

*When we pray for the Kingdom, our prayer encompasses
all we could ever need or desire because with the Kingdom
comes access to everything, all the resources of Heaven.
This is why Jesus also told us not to worry about what
we would eat, drink, or wear, or about any other thing,
but to seek first the Kingdom and righteousness of God,
for with the Kingdom comes everything else. Our future
is tied up in the culture of the King. Therefore our prayer
should be, "Lord, let Your Kingdom be manifested in
us. Make us into a community that represents Your
country and Your culture. May our common unity be
a reflection of Your glory to a watching world."*

(*God's Big Idea*, Chapter Eight)

Sincerely pray this prayer again—and commit it to
your daily devotions.

Community = Common Unity

I IN THEM AND YOU IN ME. MAY THEY BE BROUGHT TO COMPLETE UNITY TO LET THE WORLD KNOW THAT YOU SENT ME AND HAVE LOVED THEM EVEN AS YOU HAVE LOVED ME (JOHN 17:23).

MAY THE GOD WHO GIVES ENDURANCE AND ENCOURAGEMENT GIVE YOU A SPIRIT OF UNITY AMONG YOURSELVES AS YOU FOLLOW CHRIST JESUS (ROMANS 15:5).

MAKE EVERY EFFORT TO KEEP THE UNITY OF THE SPIRIT THROUGH THE BOND OF PEACE (EPHESIANS 4:3).

TODAY'S DEVOTION

Chinatown is a community. Its inhabitants are united by the common bond of their Chinese heritage and culture, which they keep vibrantly alive. Chinatown could never exist with only one or two or even a handful of Chinese. Maintaining a distinct cultural identity requires a large number of people of similar background working together in common purpose. In Los Angeles, the population of Chinatown is around 500,000 people. They speak their own language, worship in their own temples, operate their own businesses, and maintain their own distinctive cuisine. Theirs is a distinct and unmistakably unique community, a "garden" of China within the United States.

Kingdom communities, wherever they are in the world, should be just as unique and distinctive. Our values, standards, beliefs, norms, language, customs, traditions, and ideals should set us apart from the rest of the world. People who walk into our community should feel like they have stepped into Heaven.

(*God's Big Idea*, Chapter Eight)

CONSIDERATIONS

1. Why is it impossible for "religious" Christianity to take the place of the Kingdom?

2. Religious Christianity looks nothing like Heaven. Why?

3. The Kingdom of Heaven is bigger than our _____ and broader than our _____. Explain.

4. Can you envision a community on Earth where they forgive one another, love their enemies, do good to those who mistreat them, never engage in slander or gossip, are honest, and respect the dignity of others? Why or why not?

5. What must happen first before a fallen humankind can assume a common ideology, or philosophy, with the King of kings?

MEDITATION

Can you see Heaven's culture coming to Earth? Can you imagine a community where every husband loves his wife the way Christ loves His Church, and treats her like the queen she is? Can you imagine a community where every wife honors, respects, and builds up her husband? Can you imagine a community where husbands and wives are absolutely faithful to each other and where adultery or sweethearting is inconceivable? Can you imagine a community where all the children honor and obey their parents and show respect to all legitimate authority? Can you imagine a community where people's word is their bond and where honesty is the common currency? Can you imagine a community where there is no cursing or gambling, no greed or thievery, no envy or jealousy, no backbiting or backstabbing, no petty bickering or quarreling, and no lust or sexual immorality? Can you imagine a community where there is no poverty or want, but abundant peace and contentment? Can you imagine it? God can, and this is the type of community He wants to fill the Earth with.

(*God's Big Idea*, Chapter Eight)

Take a few minutes to close your eyes and imagine living in a community where God's love permeates all.

A Lesson to Learn

. . . IF YOUR PRESENCE DOES NOT GO WITH US, DO NOT SEND US UP FROM HERE. HOW WILL ANYONE KNOW THAT YOU ARE PLEASED WITH ME AND WITH YOUR PEOPLE UNLESS YOU GO WITH US? WHAT ELSE WILL DISTINGUISH ME AND YOUR PEOPLE FROM ALL THE OTHER PEOPLE ON THE FACE OF THE EARTH? (EXODUS 33:15B–16)

TODAY'S DEVOTION

If there is any group of people on Earth who understand the power of community, it is the Jews. Through 4,000 years of war and conquest, peace and prosperity, persecution and prejudice, and triumph and tragedy, the Jews have maintained a distinct cultural identity as a people. This is due in large part to the fact that they identify themselves not only as individuals but also as interdependent members of a larger community.

The first five books of the Bible are political books, not religious treatises. They explain how God's purpose for delivering the Israelites from slavery in Egypt was to transform them into a nation through whom He would bless the world, just as He had promised Abraham (see Gen. 12:1-3). According to God's plan they would be a distinct people, separate from the other nations of the world in their worship, their laws, their morality, their diet, their code of conduct, and their everyday lifestyle. The distinguishing characteristic that would set them apart from other peoples would be God's active and continuing presence among them.

(*God's Big Idea*, Chapter Eight)

CONSIDERATIONS

1. The active and powerful presence of God in our everyday lives and activities distinguishes believers from other people. How?

2. Members of Jewish communities help each other. Why don't believers and followers of Christ do the same? We have no sense of community. Why?

3. As Kingdom citizens we are a community, and we are dependent on one another. How is today's community of believers different from those of the first-century church?

4. Some communities publish directories of local and regional businesses and services owned by believers. Why should believers consider patronizing only these businesses?

5. What are some of the advantages of establishing a Christian-based community where everyone is committed to serving God and each other?

MEDITATION

As a Kingdom community, we are held to a higher standard than that of the world. Religious communities often adapt and conform to the world's standards, which is one reason they are such a mess. Kingdom communities, on the other hand, do not accommodate; they elevate. They hold out the standards of the King without compromise, and elevate to that level all who enter. That's the only way it can be. ...

In a Kingdom community, Kingdom citizens have no independent life. This is a particularly hard concept to grasp for those who have grown up under democratic and capitalistic systems where personal independence is regarded as one of the highest values of all. As Kingdom citizens, we are all in this together. We need each other. We are all members of one Body and every member is vital for the proper functioning of that Body. That is why an "illness" that infects one of us infects all of us. And that is why we cannot afford to ignore or write off any member of the community.

(*God's Big Idea*, Chapter Eight)

What lesson can you learn from the Jewish mindset about community? Think of ways you can infuse this lesson within your Christian community.

The Principle of Engagement

THEN THE RIGHTEOUS WILL ANSWER HIM, "LORD, WHEN DID WE SEE YOU HUNGRY AND FEED YOU, OR THIRSTY AND GIVE YOU SOMETHING TO DRINK? WHEN DID WE SEE YOU A STRANGER AND INVITE YOU IN, OR NEEDING CLOTHES AND CLOTHE YOU? WHEN DID WE SEE YOU SICK OR IN PRISON AND GO TO VISIT YOU?"

THE KING WILL REPLY, "I TELL YOU THE TRUTH, WHATEVER YOU DID FOR ONE OF THE LEAST OF THESE BROTHERS OF MINE, YOU DID FOR ME" (MATTHEW 25:37–40).

TODAY'S DEVOTION

We have not inherited a religion. Cultures and societies may transfer religions from one generation to the next, but that is not our inheritance. Our inheritance is the Kingdom—not just any kingdom, but *the* Kingdom. What Adam lost, Christ has restored to us. Rulership is in our genes; authority, in our very makeup. We were designed to rule the Earth. The Kingdom is the rightful inheritance of all humankind. Many people, however, do not know this, which is why we of the Kingdom community must engage those who live in the world's culture. They need to be informed of their inheritance.

As Kingdom citizens, our goal should be to stay in touch with Heaven every moment of every day. It is for this reason that God sent His Holy Spirit not to visit us but to live inside of us, so He could guide us into the knowledge of all truth and teach us how to live and act and talk like the King.

This is the way—and the only way—for us to exert a continuing influence and make a permanent impact for the Kingdom in the popular culture. In order to transform the popular culture, we must *engage* the popular culture, and we can engage it successfully only in the Spirit, likeness, and power of our King.

(*God's Big Idea*, Chapter Nine)

CONSIDERATIONS

1. "The Kingdom principle of engagement is simply defined as influencing the popular culture through the community of faith." List a few examples of how this principle can be implemented within a local community, state, and nation.

2. As Kingdom citizens and members of the Kingdom community, we not only possess the answer to humanity's search for meaning, but also bear the responsibility of sharing it with others. How have you found to be the best way to share the Good News with others?

3. Are most Christians in Western nations committed to representing the nature and character of our King, and to live His culture daily before the world with boldness and without apology or compromise?

4. The King desires for every person in the world to become a citizen of His community and receive his or her inheritance. Influencing popular culture where you live causes a wide-reaching ripple effect. How and why?

5. To transform the popular culture, we must _____ the popular culture, and we can _____ it successfully only in the Spirit, likeness, and power of our King.

```
MEDITATION
```

*Although we will not experience the complete fullness
of our inheritance until we enter the life to come, as
Kingdom citizens our inheritance is a present reality.
In fact, Kingdom community life is the daily living
out of our inheritance in real and practical ways.*

(*God's Big Idea*, Chapter Nine)

Jesus told His disciples to "feed My sheep." Think of
three ways you can feed His sheep. Choose one and
put your thoughts into action.

Heaven Is Not Our Priority (Part 1)

THE HIGHEST HEAVENS BELONG TO THE LORD, BUT THE EARTH HE HAS GIVEN TO MAN (PSALM 115:16).

TODAY'S DEVOTION

When talking about the Kingdom principle of engagement it is important first that we understand what our assignment is *not*. Because there is so much confusion on this issue, we need to be absolutely clear about what we are not supposed to do. ...

Just as Heaven is not our priority, the world is not our enemy. Although as Kingdom citizens we are not *of* the world, we are *in* the world, and it is God's will that we engage the world's culture with the principles, claims, and authority of the Kingdom of Heaven.

(*God's Big Idea*, Chapter Nine)

CONSIDERATIONS

1. *"God did not assign us to go to Heaven."* Describe your thoughts about this statement.

2. *"God did not assign us to prepare others to 'go to Heaven.'"* Describe your thoughts about this statement.

3. *"God did not assign us to establish a religion."* Describe your thoughts about this statement.

4. *"God did not assign us to promote a religion or a denomination."* Describe your thoughts about this statement.

5. *"God did not assign us to separate or isolate ourselves from the world."* Describe your thoughts about this statement.

MEDITATION

We cannot engage the popular culture by escaping from it, nor can we influence it by isolating ourselves from it. Jesus certainly didn't. One of the biggest criticisms the religious leaders leveled against Jesus was the fact that He spent so much time with "sinners," the dirty, disreputable, and cast off dregs of society. When challenged on this, He responded, "It is not the healthy who need a doctor, but the sick. But go and learn what this means: 'I desire mercy, not sacrifice.' For I have not come to call the righteous, but sinners" (Matt. 9:12-13). That is our assignment too.

(*God's Big Idea*, Chapter Nine)

Heaven is not our priority—spreading the Kingdom of God on Earth is!

Heaven Is Not Our Priority (Part 2)

THE HIGHEST HEAVENS BELONG TO THE LORD, BUT THE EARTH HE HAS GIVEN TO MAN (PSALM 115:16).

TODAY'S DEVOTION

We accomplish nothing by attacking and condemning people for their sins. Deep in their hearts, unbelievers know they are sinners. They know their lives are messed up and out of alignment with God. They don't need us in our self-righteousness laying it out for them, especially if we come off sounding like we think we are beyond those kinds of things. They know better. We can't draw people to the Kingdom by offending them with our manner. (Becoming offended by our message, however, is another matter entirely.) In order to influence them, we must show patience and sensitivity. ...

There is no need for us to "defend" the Kingdom; that is not our job. The King is perfectly capable of defending His own Kingdom. Our assignment is not to compete with the world, because there is no competition. We are from a different country than those who are of the world. Our job is not to compete, but to manifest the Kingdom in our lives, and let the Kingdom speak for itself.

(God's Big Idea, Chapter Nine)

CONSIDERATIONS

1. ***"God did not assign us to attack or condemn the world."*** Describe your thoughts about this statement.

2. ***"God did not assign us to compete with the world."*** Describe your thoughts about this statement.

3. ***"God did not assign us to avoid the world."*** Describe your thoughts about this statement.

4. Does it seem as if believers are trying to compete with the world? List several ways you've witnessed this competition.

5. Because of the escapist mentality taught by many churches, many believers have virtually written off any chance or effort of trying to change the world. Why is this reasoning faulty?

MEDITATION

As Kingdom citizens, we are in the world for a reason, not to avoid the world, but to do our part to influence and change the world through our personal involvement. Run for the school board so you can help monitor what kinds of textbooks come into the classrooms in your community. Get involved in politics. Run for office, or at the very least, vote regularly. Read up on current issues and stay abreast of the news. Choose a "secular" career that will get you into the mainstream of society where your influence can be the greatest. Get involved in education. Get involved in business. Get involved in entertainment. Get involved in every area of law and medicine. We cannot engage the popular culture by avoiding it; we must fill it with Kingdom people.

(*God's Big Idea*, Chapter Nine)

Is God calling you to step out into a new area for Him? Trust that He will give you all the talent, skill, and encouragement you need to succeed!

Engaging the World

YOU ARE THE SALT OF THE EARTH. BUT IF THE SALT LOSES ITS SALTINESS, HOW CAN IT BE MADE SALTY AGAIN? IT IS NO LONGER GOOD FOR ANYTHING, EXCEPT TO BE THROWN OUT AND TRAMPLED BY MEN.

YOU ARE THE LIGHT OF THE WORLD. A CITY SET ON A HILL CANNOT BE HIDDEN. NEITHER DO PEOPLE LIGHT A LAMP AND PUT IT UNDER A BOWL. INSTEAD THEY PUT IT ON ITS STAND, AND IT GIVES LIGHT TO EVERYONE IN THE HOUSE. IN THE SAME WAY, LET YOUR LIGHT SHINE BEFORE MEN, THAT THEY MAY SEE YOUR GOOD DEEDS AND PRAISE YOUR FATHER IN HEAVEN (MATTHEW 5:13–16).

God did not place us on Earth as His people just so we could start getting ready to leave. He placed us here to plant and reproduce gardens of His Kingdom throughout the world, thereby reclaiming and transforming territory laid waste by the pretender's rapacious rule. ...

Religion separates and isolates. The Kingdom engages. Just as a farmer sows his seed, so the King sprinkles His Kingdom citizens everywhere with an abundant harvest in mind. He is saying, "I am throwing you out; wherever you land, infect that place for Me. Don't isolate yourself. Don't stay away from folks who are not in the Kingdom. Get involved. Engage. Make an impact where you are. Be bold in My strength to confront the earthly powers of this present age. The world will soon see who is more powerful." The Kingdom of Heaven is not afraid of evil, and we who are its citizens need not fear it either, because the One who is in us is greater than the one who is in the world (see 1 John 4:4).

(*God's Big Idea*, Chapter Nine)

CONSIDERATIONS

1. Write a brief thought about each of the following statements:
   God assigned us to reintroduce the Kingdom to the world.

   God assigned us to repossess the Earth with the Kingdom.

   God assigned us to engage the world system.

   God assigned us to influence the world, not to keep up with it.

2. Write a brief thought about each of the following statements:
   God assigned us to infect the world, not reject the world.

   God assigned us to revolutionize the world.

   God assigned us to occupy the Earth, not abandon it.

   God assigned us to promote the government of Heaven on Earth.

MEDITATION

As Jesus explained to His disciples later, the man who sowed the good seed represents the Son of Man, Jesus Himself; the enemy who sowed the weeds is the devil; the good seed represents children of the Kingdom, and the weeds, children of the devil (see Matt. 13:37-39).

*The point I want us to understand here is that the wheat and the weeds—the children of the Kingdom and the children of the devil—are allowed to **grow together** until the harvest, which is the end of time. In other words, Kingdom citizens **mingle** with citizens of the world throughout history, and this is by the King's design. He has chosen deliberately to leave His children in the world, in the midst of the "weeds," so that we can make a difference in the lives of those weeds.*

In strictly human terms, we all know that a weed cannot change into a stalk of wheat, but in God's Kingdom nothing is impossible. By His power working in and through the lives and influence of His people, God can convert useless weeds into purposeful wheat. He can transform dark, confused, broken, and unproductive people into persons full of purpose, abundant life, and fulfilled destiny. But He cannot work through us for this purpose unless we are in the world and among the weeds. That is the concept behind the Kingdom principle of engagement.

(*God's Big Idea*, Chapter Nine)

How willing are you to engage some weeds for the purpose of establishing His Garden?

Living in Two Worlds

YOUR KINGDOM IS AN EVERLASTING KINGDOM,
AND YOUR DOMINION ENDURES THROUGH ALL
GENERATIONS (PSALM 145:13A).

TODAY'S DEVOTION

Kingdom citizens are people with their feet in two different worlds. One foot is planted squarely in the Kingdom community, where daily life is ordered by the righteous principles, standards, and culture of God Almighty, while the other stands securely in the society and culture of the world. At heart, the two worlds are incompatible because they operate according to principles and philosophies that are diametrically opposed to each other. Yet we live in both worlds simultaneously. This is the challenge of living in the Kingdom. In order to do so successfully, we have to understand the principle of Kingdom extension and influence and how it works in counterculture with the present culture we are in. How do we live in two worlds on one Earth? More importantly, how do we claim one world—the popular culture—and bring it under Kingdom government?

Attitude is the key, and attitude determines strategy.

(*God's Big Idea,* Chapter Ten)

CONSIDERATIONS

1. List a few times when you felt as if you had one foot in the Kingdom of Heaven and the other foot in the world's kingdom.

2. "Whenever we pray, 'Your kingdom come, and Your will be done on earth as it is in heaven,' we are praying for the celestial to transform the terrestrial." Describe what this means to you.

3. As children of God created in His image and likeness, we have firm connections to the celestial and the terrestrial. How do these connections enhance or detract from our connection with God?

4. "One of the first attitude adjustments we must make is to get rid of our 'religious' thinking." Why?

5. In what ways can believers prepare themselves for the inevitable clash of the two worlds they live in?

MEDITATION

*All who are Kingdom citizens face the dilemma and
challenge of how to live successfully and simultaneously
in two worlds that are in inevitable conflict. In Chapter Two
we talked about the clash of cultures between the Kingdom
and the world. One critical key to our successful navigation
within these two worlds is to get it thoroughly into our heads
that the Kingdom of Heaven is not a kingdom of coexistence
but of transformation, and that it is the Kingdom, not the
world, that will ultimately prevail. This understanding can
help us develop the habit of thinking with a Kingdom
mindset and making Kingdom decisions in every area of life.*

*As Kingdom citizens, we must be prepared for clash
and conflict. We cannot enter the Kingdom of God and
continue to live like our unsaved friends. All of a sudden
everything changes: our culture, our nature, our interests,
our priorities, our tastes—everything. We are new creations
in Christ; the old is gone and everything has become new
(see 2 Cor. 5:17). Our assignment on Earth is not
coexistence, compromise, or half measures. It is total
transformation. It is love taking over a love-starved planet.*

(*God's Big Idea*, Chapter Ten)

Most people try to avoid conflict—are you prepared
for the inevitable?

Transformation

Do not conform any longer to the pattern of this world, but be transformed by the renewing of your mind (ROMANS 12:2A).

TODAY'S DEVOTION

Whenever the Kingdom comes into a place, it impacts and overrides the culture of that place, not with violence or heavy-handed tactics, but with love and an unshakable confidence in the absolute legitimacy, superiority, and supremacy of Kingdom government. We are not supposed to dress like the popular culture, or live like the popular culture, or take a light view of sex and morality like the popular culture. We are supposed to set the standard, the higher standard of the Kingdom. We are supposed to override the popular culture. We are supposed to exercise self-control and moderation in all things and impact the people around us. We should not allow the environment to change us.

Instead, we should change our environment and bring it into conformity with God's Kingdom. The apostle Paul said, "Do not conform any longer to the pattern of this world, but be transformed by the renewing of your mind" (Rom. 12:2a). Once transformed in this manner, we then transform our environment wherever we go until it is a clear reflection of the Kingdom.

(*God's Big Idea*, Chapter Ten)

DAY 38—*Transformation*

CONSIDERATIONS

1. Fill in the blanks according to the differences between God's Kingdom and the kingdom of the world:

God's Kingdom	world's kingdom
Sexual purity	Immorality
Respect	_____
Order	_____
Honesty	_____
Truthfulness	_____
Love	_____
Peace	_____
Freedom	_____

2. Transformation of the popular culture will come only from communities of Kingdom citizens who refuse to remain silent. What are two topics you can speak out about and make a positive difference?

3. "We must become proactive in reproducing Garden communities of the Kingdom wherever we are and wherever we go in the future." How will today's Garden communities be different from the Garden of Eden?

4. In Chapter Ten's example about the manager who turned a failing restaurant into a success, name five things that she did to transform the business. Were lives transformed as well? Who and why?

5. Transformation begins with you. How can you transform yourself, your family, your neighborhood, your church, your state, and your nation for His glory? Write at least one idea for each area.

MEDITATION

No coexistence. Transformation of the popular culture will come only from communities of Kingdom citizens who refuse to remain silent; who refuse to sit idly by, uninvolved and disengaged, while the agents of the "powers of this dark world and…the spiritual forces of evil in the heavenly realms" (Eph. 6:12) set their agenda and run the show. We must speak up. We must step out. We must get involved. We must become proactive in reproducing garden communities of the Kingdom wherever we are and wherever we go in the future. That is our calling, and our assignment from the One who commanded us to "go and make disciples of all nations, baptizing them in the name of the Father and of the Son and of the Holy Spirit, and teaching them to obey everything I have commanded you" (Matt. 28:19-20a).

(*God's Big Idea*, Chapter Ten)

Transforming from inside out is the biggest challenge—start today.

Then start outside tomorrow.

DAY 39

A Just and Righteous King

N O GOOD TREE BEARS BAD FRUIT, NOR DOES A BAD TREE BEAR GOOD FRUIT. EACH TREE IS RECOGNIZED BY ITS OWN FRUIT. PEOPLE DO NOT PICK FIGS FROM THORNBUSHES, OR GRAPES FROM BRIERS. THE GOOD MAN BRINGS GOOD THINGS OUT OF THE GOOD STORED UP IN HIS HEART, AND THE EVIL MAN BRINGS EVIL THINGS OUT OF THE EVIL STORED UP IN HIS HEART. FOR OUT OF THE OVERFLOW OF HIS HEART HIS MOUTH SPEAKS (LUKE 6:43–45).

$$\boxed{\text{TODAY'S DEVOTION}}$$

Human history is replete with examples of good kings and bad kings, good kingdoms and bad kingdoms, benevolent governments and oppressive governments. One fact that stands out clearly is this: As the king goes, so goes the kingdom. Since a kingdom is tied so closely to the nature and character of its king, it is virtually impossible for a good kingdom to come from a bad king, or a bad kingdom to come from a good king. ...

Fortunately for all of us, the King of kings is a good King, and His Kingdom is a good kingdom. That is why we who are citizens of the Kingdom of Heaven can live and work for the Kingdom—and engage the popular culture with it—in complete confidence that we are serving not only God, but also the better interests of our fellow humans who are not yet in the Kingdom. Our King's rule is just and righteous. He rules with fairness, grace, compassion, mercy, and, most of all, love. And in His love He delights to give all good things to His children, His people.

(*God's Big Idea*, Chapter Ten)

CONSIDERATIONS

1. How does our King of kings differ from kings of this world, be they unscrupulous CEOs, territorial dictators, dishonest managers, drunken husbands, etc.?

2. Jesus said, "Do not be afraid, little flock, for your Father has been pleased to give you the kingdom." Why did He preface His statement with "Do not be afraid"? What are people afraid of?

3. A depraved king's kingdom will be characterized by _____ , _____ , and _____.

4. The wealth of a kingdom will be reflected in the lifestyle of its people. If the kingdom is rich and the king is good, the people will be well off. Describe your lifestyle and quality of life as a citizen of the Kingdom of God.

5. Jesus says to you, "Come to Me, all you who are weary and burdened, and I will give you rest. Take My yoke upon you and learn from Me, for I am gentle and humble in heart, and you will find rest for your souls. For My yoke is easy and My burden is light" (Matt. 11:28-30). Does this Scripture bring you peace and comfort? Write about it.

MEDITATION

The King has the power and the ability to give rest to everyone who comes to Him—including all 6 billion plus of us on the face of the Earth. This is not some sweet and sentimental religious statement; it is a legal Kingdom decree. "Come to Me, all six billion and more of you; I can heal you all, house you all, feed you all, dress you all, and bless you all—and still have as much resources as when I began."

Jesus is a good King, and His Kingdom is just what the world needs, which is why He wants to fill the Earth with His Kingdom communities, and use His citizens to do it.

(*God's Big Idea*, Chapter Ten)

Living for a just and righteous King gives you purpose, hope, and lasting joy. Start living for Him today.

Victory Through Service

J ESUS SAID TO THEM, "YOU WILL INDEED DRINK FROM MY CUP, BUT TO SIT AT MY RIGHT OR LEFT IS NOT FOR ME TO GRANT. THESE PLACES BELONG TO THOSE FOR WHOM THEY HAVE BEEN PREPARED BY MY FATHER."

WHEN THE TEN HEARD ABOUT THIS, THEY WERE INDIGNANT WITH THE TWO BROTHERS. JESUS CALLED THEM TOGETHER AND SAID, "YOU KNOW THAT THE RULERS OF THE GENTILES LORD IT OVER THEM, AND THEIR HIGH OFFICIALS EXERCISE AUTHORITY OVER THEM. NOT SO WITH YOU. INSTEAD, WHOEVER WANTS TO BECOME GREAT AMONG YOU MUST BE YOUR SER-VANT, AND WHOEVER WANTS TO BE FIRST MUST BE YOUR SLAVE—JUST AS THE SON OF MAN DID NOT COME TO BE SERVED, BUT TO SERVE, AND TO GIVE HIS LIFE AS A RANSOM FOR MANY" (MATTHEW 20:23-28).

TODAY'S DEVOTION

"The Son of Man did not come to be served, but to serve, and to give His life as a ransom for many." Notice the progression here: Jesus became a servant, and then He gave Himself. By His example He is telling us: "Find your gift and serve it to the world. That is how you will infect people with the Kingdom." If you set your heart on the Kingdom of Heaven and your sights on serving others in the King's name, He will open doors of opportunity for you that would never open otherwise. He will take you to places you would never be able to go on your own, and enable you to impact lives you would never even come close to touching any other way. He will take you to personal heights of joy, prosperity, and contentment beyond your wildest dreams and give you a broader influence in your world than you have ever imagined. But those things come not by seeking them, but by seeking Him; not by seeking the gifts, but by seeking the Giver.

(*God's Big Idea*, Chapter Ten)

DAY 40—*Victory Through Service*

CONSIDERATIONS

1. To expand God's Kingdom, believers must not use tactics of the world such self-promotion or selfish ambition. What principles should we use instead?

2. Define *self-abasement* and *servanthood.*

3. List five things that will happen if you set your heart on the Kingdom of Heaven and your sights on serving others in the King's name:

4. Setting aside your own ambitions and surrendering to His will for your life opens opportunities you never imagined. Do you have a secret desire that God has placed in your heart? Write it down.

5. *"Every good and perfect gift is from above, coming down from the Father of the heavenly lights, who does not change like shifting shadows"* (James 1:17). Discover, define, and refine your gift from God—then give it away as part of planting His gardens.

   Describe the gift(s) God has given you to share with others.

MEDITATION

Everyone dreams of being great, and there is nothing evil in that desire. We all want to be part of something significant. This is perfectly natural. Such a desire comes from God, because He created us for greatness, but we lost it when we lost the Kingdom. We can get it back, but not by walking on top of people, pushing people down, lording it over people, conniving, scheming, lying, stealing, or dealing under the table. Those are the ways of the world. In God's Kingdom, if you want to be great, you first must become the servant of all. …

God's big idea was to extend His kingly influence and culture from the celestial to the terrestrial by planting garden communities throughout the Earth that would perfectly reflect the richness and abundant life of His heavenly Kingdom. And He chose to do it through citizen-servants like you and me who will seek first His Kingdom and His righteousness and live exclusively for Him by humbling ourselves and giving ourselves freely to others so that they may see Him in us, learn of His Kingdom from us, and apply for citizenship themselves.

(*God's Big Idea,* Chapter Ten)

God's big idea includes you!

Accept His invitation to become the royal heir of His Kingdom, now and forever.

Bahamas Faith Ministries International

The Diplomat Center

Carmichael Road

P.O. Box N-9583

Nassau, Bahamas

Tel 242-341-6444

Fax 242-361-2260

Website: http://www.bfmmm.com

Made in United States
Orlando, FL
11 February 2022